CONCILIUM

CONCILIUM
ADVISORY COMMITTEE

Gregory Baum	Montreal, QC Canada
José Oscar Beozzo	São Paulo, SP Brazil
Wim Beuken	Louvain Belgium
Leonardo Boff	Petrópolis, RJ Brazil
John Coleman	Los Angeles, CA USA
Christian Duquoc	Lyon France
Virgil Elizondo	San Antonio, TX USA
Sean Freyne	Dublin Ireland
Claude Geffré	Paris France
Norbert Greinacher	Tübingen Germany
Gustavo Gutiérrez	Lima Peru
Hermann Häring	Tübingen Germany
Werner G. Jeanrond	Glasgow Scotland
Jean-Pierre Jossua	Paris France
Maureen Junker-Kenny	Dublin Ireland
François Kabasele Lumbala	Kinshasa Dem. Rep. of Congo
Nicholas Lash	Cambridge England
Mary-John Mananzan	Manila Philippines
Alberto Melloni	Reggio Emilia Italy
Norbert Mette	Münster Germany
Dietmar Mieth	Tübingen Germany
Jürgen Moltmann	Tübingen Germany
Teresa Okure	Port Harcourt Nigeria
Aloysius Pieris	Kelaniya, Colombo Sri Lanka
David Power	Washington, D.C. USA
Giuseppe Ruggieri	Catania Italy
Paul Schotsmans	Louvain Belgium
Janet Martin Soskice	Cambridge England
Elsa Tamez	San José Costa Rica
Christoph Theobald	Paris France
David Tracy	Chicago, IL USA
Marciano Vidal	Madrid Spain
Ellen van Wolde	Tilburg Holland

CONCILIUM 2012/4

GENDER IN THEOLOGY, SPIRITUALITY AND PRACTICE

Edited by

Lisa Sowle Cahill, Diego Irarrazaval
and Elaine M. Wainwright

SCM Press · London

Published in 2012 by SCM Press, 3rd Floor, Invicta House, 108–114 Golden Lane, London EC1Y 0TG.

SCM Press is an imprint of Hymns Ancient & Modern Ltd (a registered charity) 13A Hellesdon Park Road, Norwich NR6 5DR, UK

Copyright © International Association of Conciliar Theology, Madras (India)

www.concilium.in

English translations copyright © 2012 Hymns Ancient & Modern Ltd.

All rights reserved. No part of this publication may be reproduced, stored in a retrieval system, or transmitted, in any form or by any means, electronic, mechanical, photocopying or otherwise, without the prior written permission of the Board of Directors of Concilium.

ISBN 9780334031208

Printed in the UK by
CPI Antony Rowe, Chippenham, Wiltshire

Concilium is published in March, June, August, October, December

Contents

Editorial
Gender and Theology: Introduction 7

Part One: Contexts

Dangerous Thinking. Gender and Theology 13
REGINA AMMICHT QUINN

Gender, Politics and the Catholic Church 26
REBEKA JADRANKA ANIĆ

Theology in the Context of Reciprocity and Complementarity
   between Men and Women 36
BENDITO FERRARO

The Language of Creation and Gender 46
LUIS CORRÉA LIMA SJ

Creation: God, Humans and the Natural World 56
HEATHER EATON

Torah for Women, Confusing Relations and a Winged Deity 67
MARIE-THERES WACKER

Women's Leadership in the New Testament 77
ELSA TAMEZ

Revisiting and Reclaiming Incarnation: An Asian Woman's
   Christological Journey 86
MURIEL OREVILLO-MONTENEGRO

The Trinity: Gender and the Role of Dissonance 95
PATRICIA A. FOX

Liberating Renunciation: Contemporary Feminist Spirituality 102
SUSAN M. ST VILLE

Gender and Ecclesiology: Authorities, Structures, Ministry 110
ANNE ARABOME SSS

Part Two: Theological Forum

The Elizabeth A. Johnson Case in the United States 121
BRADFORD E. HINZE & CHRISTINE FIRER HINZE

What is Reality?: Situating an Ontological Question 126
PAULO SUESS

The Arab Spring: Arab Non-violence as a Sign of the Times 131
DREW CHRISTIANSEN SJ

Contributors 136

Editorial
Gender and Theology: Introduction

Today most of the world's Christians agree that women and men are equally made in the image of God and equally redeemed in Christ. Most Christians also know that God is beyond time and space and, while imagined as a 'Father', is not literally a male. The great Trinitarian and Christological councils of Nicaea (325 CE) and Chalcedon (451 CE) make Jesus' humanity essential to his saving role, and clearly recognize that Jesus of Nazareth was a man. But they never suggest that it is Christ's maleness (rather than his humanity) that unites humans with God in a saving way. Jesus' inclusive ministry of the reign of God challenged many of the gender stereotypes of his day, as well as customary strictures on women. Even though the early Church incorporated vestiges of the patriarchal Greek 'household codes' into Scripture, an inclusive ideal of Church still shines through all this: 'There is neither Jew nor Greek, slave nor free, male nor female, for you are all one in Christ Jesus' (Gal. 3.28).

Nevertheless, the historic Christian churches with their theologies, spiritualities, and practices have often interpreted God and salvation in ways that are gender-biased, and have worked particularly to the detriment of women. For this reason, in his 1995 *Letter to Women*, John Paul II found it necessary to say that women's dignity had often been unacknowledged and their prerogatives misrepresented: '…they have often been relegated to the margins of society and even reduced to servitude…And if objective blame, especially in particular historical contexts, has belonged to not just a few members of the Church, for this I am truly sorry' (3).

Gender stereotypes also harm the full humanity of men, forcing them into socially-constructed 'masculinities' that provide a mirror image of female oppression. Today both masculinity and femininity are problematized, and the model of gender complementarity is interrogated, in practice and theory.

Editorial

This number of *Concilium* will consider the implicit and explicit roles that gender has played, and still plays, in the Christian theological tradition, influencing the composition and interpretation of Scripture, the formulation of theological doctrines, the shaping of Christian spiritualities, and the vision of the Church both as an institution and as comprising local communities and lay leadership.

An introductory essay by Regina Ammicht Quinn addresses the distinction of and relation between sex and gender, and reminds us that unmasking gender ideologies is dangerous. Tensions in the very communities that produced the biblical texts, as well as in every community that reads them, are illustrated by Elsa Tamez's essay on women's leadership in the New Testament, and by Marie-Theres Wacker's exploration of the biblical narrative of Ruth. The actual suffering of women in the most acute situations of gender oppression comes through powerfully in the essay by Anne Arabome on women's roles in Church and society, especially in the global south. Rebeka Anic explores the politics of gender as reflected in recent papal and episcopal documents. Luis Corrêa Lima avoids binary categories in order to show the relevance of gender difference to sex, heterosexuality and homosexuality.

Nevertheless, the aim of this issue is not simply to provide an overview of relevant topics. Rather, authors were invited to take up new or cutting-edge issues, and to provide creative suggestions from a variety of cultural and regional contexts. This issue of *Concilium* has not been designed to present a unitary view, to represent the opinions of the editors, or to avoid controversy. We trust readers will find that it offers innovative thinking and enables them to reach a new appreciation of the 'diverse and manifold ways' (International Theological Commission, *Theology Today: Perspectives, Principles and Criteria*, November 2011) in which theology approaches the mystery of God.

As Patricia Fox argues, a certain 'cognitive dissonance' in theology reminds us of God's infinity and incomprehensibility. Yet theological dissonance invites disagreement and even rejection. That creativity and pluralism bring risks is evident in debates about the feminist theology of Elizabeth Johnson, discussed in the 'Theological Forum' in this issue. Almost all readers of this issue of *Concilium* will find that it contains something provocative and even 'beyond the boundaries'.

For those committed to gender equality, it may be Benedito Ferraro's attempt to retrieve gender 'complementarity and reciprocity' in a way

Editorial

consistent with feminism. Or it may be Susan St Ville's attempt to understand why some abused women embrace a spirituality of 'surrender'. Those who prioritize the Christological hermeneutics of Nicaea and Chalcedon will be equally challenged by Heather Eaton's reinterpretations of divine immanence and eternal life; Muriel Orevillo's consideration whether the Spirit may empower new incarnations of the divine; and Paulo Suess's perception that official church teachers do not always grasp 'reality' appropriately. Finally, writing in the 'Theological Forum' on a different topic, the 'Arab Spring', Drew Christiansen shows that unexpected historical developments and even radical changes can be signs of the Spirit in history and seeds of hope for a better future.

Lisa Sowle Cahill, Diego Irarrazaval, Elaine M. Wainwright

Part One: Contexts

Dangerous Thinking
Gender and Theology

REGINA AMMICHT QUINN

I Pregnant with gender history

Tertullian was one of the first great theologians of inculturation. He was the son of a Roman officer and was born in Carthage in about 150 AD. He was the first Father of the Church to write in Latin and had a decisive influence on many later intellectual movements in Christianity. His topics included not only the Trinity, death and hell but contemporary women's fashion, which he observed very accurately. Today, his *De cultu feminarum* (On Female Fashion) is a source not only for theologians but for cultural anthropologists interested in dress and cosmetics in classical antiquity.

It is scarcely surprising that Tertullian, who died in 235 AD and was writing at a time when he might possibly have suffered martyrdom, should have condemned women who wore a lot of jewellery and make-up. What he actually said is less interesting than the rhetoric of his theological discourse.

He maintained that all women were permanently pregnant in the sense that they bore the burden of ignominy derived from Eve and the odium associated with her as the cause of human perdition: 'Do you not know that you are (each) an Eve? The sentence of God on this sex of yours lives in this age: the guilt must of necessity live too. *You* are the devil's gateway: *you* are the unsealer of that (forbidden) tree: *you* are the first deserter of the divine law: *you* are she who persuaded him whom the devil was not valiant enough to attack. *You* destroyed so easily God's image, man. On account of *your* desert — that is, death — even the Son of God had to die. And do you think about adorning yourself over and above your tunics of skins?'[1] Furthermore, each woman who is pregnant with the weight of her own sexual history is a living corpse, for her adornments 'are all the baggage of woman in her condemned and dead state, instituted as if to swell the pomp of her funeral'.[2]

These are more than just harsh words. They are examples of a 'gender theology' in which a theological interpretament (or explanatory instrument), in this case the Fall, is reconstructed and, as it were, updated using gender categories.

What does it mean to talk now, almost 2000 years later, about gender and theology? It does not mean that we are engaged in feminist theology, but in a somewhat more modern context. It does mean that 'religion' (in this case in particular a religion with a tradition as rich as that of Christianity or the traditions of the other monotheistic religions) provides a symbolic matrix within which questions of gender have always been treated as moral questions, and are still treated in that way. Theological discourse is involved with gender categories even when it isn't concerned with them.

Nowadays, doing theology using gender as a category means including the category of gender as an explicit critical category in theological discourse. That opens up new questions and lines of thought, and 'gender' runs the risk of being superseded as an uncritical category applied within theology without sufficient theoretical reflection.

The category of gender has its own modern history of reference to the contexts of feminist theologies.

II Equality, difference, diversity

As far as the European and North American context is concerned, feminist theology is historically indebted to the secular women's movement of the nineteenth and twentieth centuries.

This secular political women's movement can be shown to have had three phases, which do not divide cleanly but overlap with and exist alongside each other. The watchword of the first phase was 'equality'. It saw the rise of the first women's movement in the mid-nineteenth century with the struggle for equal rights and for the same access to education, to political co-determination and to offices of all kinds. The second phase began with the new women's movement of the 1970s in Western industrialized countries. In this case, it is no longer primarily a question of equality but of difference, of the creation of spaces identified with women, which make it possible to perceive and prize what is one's own as one's own. Here we also find the origin of identity politics, which sees a uniformly conceived gender identity as a presupposition of political emancipation.

Other phases were important and necessary. But both phases (that of equality and that of difference) become problematical as soon as they are posited absolutely. They both refer to a dichotomous reality, in which mind and body, culture and nature, reason and feeling are opposed to each other, like order and chaos, rational and irrational, and so on, and recently the terms 'man' and 'woman'. This split is both hierarchized and sexualized, for mind, culture, understanding and so forth tend to be thought of as 'better' than body, nature and feeling. At the same time, these terms and everyday realities are prone to association with male or female connotations. Discourse about equality retains hierarchization (understanding is superior to feeling, and culture to nature) but rejects sexualization (women too are capable of rational thought and discourse). There is a link here with the reason exalted by the Enlightenment, but there is also the danger of adaptation to ruling political, social but also philosophical complexes without analyzing and questioning them. Discourse about difference retains sexualization (women are more inclined than men to feeling, the body and nature), but revalues hierarchization, giving rise to a world of female otherness and female self-consciousness. But this newly-fashioned world constantly runs the risk of accepting female virtues as compensation for a lack of female rights.

A third phase of theory formation that is now called for is analysing and criticizing this dichotomy of the world of thinking and living. In so doing, it concentrates on the question of gender. A shift of emphasis and a further development are now taking place in contradistinction to the original feminist theorizing. It is no longer primarily a matter of continued criticism of the disadvantages of (Western) women. The experiences of 'white ladies' and those of most women in poor countries cannot simply be subsumed under 'women's experiences'. Over the last two decades, there has been a considerable manifestation of such new efforts as Latina theology,[3] Mujerista theology[4] and Africana theology[5] but also queer theology,[6] which have turned feminist theology into a chorus of different voices.

The aim of gender discourse is a critical analysis of power mechanisms at the basis of the separation, hierarchization and sexualization of experiential and conceptual worlds, and concern both genders. In this respect, Elisabeth Schüssler Fiorenza's 'kyriarchate' is an analytical category that makes it possible to locate gender contrasts in another context: 'It is the Western, privileged, educated male who has practised scholarship and science and has insisted that only his interpretation of the world is true and accurate. This makes knowledge itself not only gender-specific but racist, Eurocentric and class-bound.'[7] The scientific image of theories which are contradicted by new theories is inappropriate to the different stages of theological and secular consideration of gender(s). What is developing instead is a field of discourse that keeps in touch with its origins and original questions. The discursive field of gender theory advances beyond discussion of equality and difference to express a fundamental concern with the analysis and criticism of dualistic structures that are both sexualized and hierarchized. How do these structures originate, what influence do they exert, and what power is as it were ascribed to them? There is an underlying phenomenon here that has developed from the original questions of feminist discourse: an attempt to come to grips with the question of the 'other(s)', and to confront self-perceptions and perceptions of others, as well as delimitation and exclusion mechanisms. There are questions about people and groups of people that escape the confines of the soft 'female' categories and are classified as 'other(s)'.

The discursive field of gender theories shows that questions of equality persist as questions of justice for women in issues of just work, due participation, fair recognition, and just education. It shows that questions of differences continue in discussions about women's history and women's narratives. This persistence is clear where different claims and self-images come into contact, and where, for example, family and maternal images with a religious emphasis have to be reconciled with the demands of the labour market, or where equality in the realm of politics is mixed up with inequality in the private sphere.[8]

In particular, this discursive field shows that the use of an explicit and critical gender category within theology means that:
    the problems addressed are not 'women problems';
    the problems addressed cannot be solved by recourse to 'nature';
    the problems addressed cannot be solved on a Eurocentric basis.

Gender is not a 'pure theory' but 'intersectional'.[9] It comprises elements of feminist theory formation, discourse about sex and the body, queer studies, maleness studies, and diversity studies.

III Woman at home, man in the world

Gender categories are concerned neither with 'women problems' nor with Eurocentric problems. 'Doing gender' in the context of theology is *not* something that (some) women do and (some) men observe with a certain degree of goodwill, just as one watches children at play. Moreover, 'gender' is *not* something that concerns women and not men, as if women had a gender and men were neuter.

At the time of the European Enlightenment, from about 1680 to 1730, economic, scientific, political and geographical changes gave rise to a middle-class (or bourgeois) public, and an associated extensive transformation of values that emphasized reason, education, equality and humanity but had its own specific dialectic.

The process by which the middle-class public developed was linked to the process of development of an individual's privacy. With the disappearance of the whole extended household as previously conceived, the family lost its political function (as the birthplace of privilege-based class rule) and its economic function (as the locus of productive labour). Instead, it became a 'nuclear family', and the household was transformed into a 'household of sensibility or feeling', which received and nurtured the feelings now out of place in the public realm. The potential equality of all human beings is the watchword of the public sphere – which needs the private sphere as its basis and support. Here the father's rule is responsible for holding the world together, precisely when the rule of the sovereign and that of God the Father are called in question.[10]

This gradually-emerging gulf between a public and a private sphere gives rise to a new gender order, within which a woman belongs to a man's private sphere. Freedom and equality terminate at the threshold of the home, and quite complicated and reciprocal dependency relations can ensue in the house, where men not infrequently assume the part of an additional child.

The 'world' makes power relations long, or still, denied to women possible for men. But a gender theory which arranges men and women on no more than a scale of actors and victims, power and impotence is inadequate.

Maleness and power are still attributed, and the opposite is simultaneously true. Something else applies too in Germany and most Western countries. Men are not only educational failures. They represent two-thirds of all emergency patients, three-quarters of all murder victims, two-thirds of all those repeating the same class level in schools, and three-quarters of all suicides. Their life expectancy is eight years less than that of women. They suffer five times more often from heart attacks and three times more often from lung cancer. The ratio of men to women in prisons is 25:1.

More than 20 years ago, Herb Goldberg described the still relevant code of masculinity:[11] people are more masculine the more pain they suffer, the more alcohol they drink, and the less sleep they need. The less often they ask for help, the stronger they are and the more effectively they control their feelings. The fact that certain individuals reject these tendencies does not disprove the existence of a cultural environment that makes them possible.

There are other codes among women which are discussed more publicly and offensively. Contemporary culture, which produces and fosters these gender codes, also makes a space available where all these diverse practices and ideas interact. One thing is evident in these variegated mixtures: the more unambiguous and normative the gender codes are, the more problematical they become.

IV Gender means dangerous thinking

There is considerable resistance to gender questions, especially in church contexts. They are seen as ideological and therefore as dangerous. They are indeed dangerous. Thinking with the help of critical gender categories is dangerous. But it is not so because of the production of ideologies, but because it lays bare ideologies. It is a dangerous undertaking to call in question self-evident certainties or naturally-given truths. That has not escaped people's attention, and not only since Giordano Bruno.

In a gender context, naturally-given truths often assume a specific form. They are not cast in the insulting phraseology of a Tertullian but in respectful terms: men and women are equal, intellectually and spiritually. But biological differences lead to psycho-social characteristics, so that women and men are equal but different. The value and dignity of each specific sexual nature are disclosed in this kind of complementary way of being different.

V Sexual 'nature'

Nevertheless, the question of a sexual 'nature' is especially delicate and closely bound up with theological certainties, from which we must first remove the individual layers of cultural certainties carefully and earnestly.

Theological complementarity theories strike a response and find support in (popular) sociobiology from Wilson to Dawkins. New theses in this regard constantly link male dominance and female caring and compassion with forms of human reproduction and give them a biological basis. Here scientific research and a rhetoric of apology or even fear are closely interlocked. 'We can't do anything about it', is the message, 'because Mother Nature is sexist!'[12] The right and left halves of the brain, the motility and plain numerical superiority of sperm, hormonal influences, and of course physical size and strength, are juggled with and displayed in ever-new patterns. These are all assembled to show that the old socio-cultural patterns should not only be kept just as they are, but can't be changed anyway.

These are symptoms of a tunnel vision blind to cultural patterns or the interdependence between such forms and societal dynamics. The question of 'nature' is treated with an enviable lack of ambiguity. This kind of specificity asserts that there are men and women with different sexual organs for procreation or for the carrying, bearing and breast-feeding of children and the virtues which each requires for these purposes. Nowadays, however, this kind of simplistic assertion automatically attracts a whole range of queries. Ethnological, medico-historical, medical, biological and evolutionary-biological research shows clearly that sexual 'nature' is far from unambiguous.

My first example illustrates the unambiguous v. ambiguous nature of gender in certain socio-cultural contexts. Most of us are acquainted with cultural and historically-conditioned circumstances in which the dual-gender model operates as the basis of gender roles and gender conditions. It is also the basis of a constitutive world-view in which the 'man' and 'woman' dualism coexists with other dualisms such as right and left, up and down, black and white, and is taken for granted as enjoying the same specificity. This prevents us from seeing simple things: for instance, the fact that in other cultures in the world, such as those of the Pacific area, there are more than two sexes.

A case in point is that of the Fa'afafine of Samoa, who are individuals with male external sex organs, who are not defined as male because of those gender characteristics but inhabit an 'intermediate' space.[13] In general, Fa'fafine, who are 'acknowledged' either in infancy or at the beginning of puberty, think of themselves as 'born like that'. They enjoy great freedom. They can hang out with boys and men outside the village and go hunting with them; but they can also weave and cook with their sisters and sleep in the women's quarters. Some of them wear male clothing and others women's dress. They can marry women and live married lives or look for men as sexual partners. They often play an important part in the local church communities, but just as often they suffer discrimination as a consequence of Christianization, which labels the defenceless Fa'afafine 'homosexuals'.

The second example comes from the analysis of traditional Western culture. Here, too, 'sexual nature' is not so straightforward and unambiguous as it appears. According to Thomas Laqueur,[14] from antiquity until the eighteenth century there was only a single normative culture; only a single normative body, the male body; and only a single normative gender, the male gender. The male body is the human body. In this view, women are located on a vertical axis as lower, inferior versions of the one male gender; and women are imperfect men. In fact, they possess the same genitals as men but their imperfection (which Aristotle attributes to a lack of vital heat) has caused those essential structures to be retained within. Therefore female genitals are as it were 'unborn' male genitals: the vagina an inner, less perfect penis, the labia the foreskin, the uterus the scrotum, and the ovaries the testicles. There are no male and female genitals but only perfect and imperfect male genitals; perfect genitals make a person a man and imperfect genitals make a person a woman.

Then (around the eighteenth century), human 'nature' changed. A new model came into existence: the 'dual-gender / dual-body model'.[15] This model was based on the radical contrast between men and women, and on an anatomy of incomparability. The sexes were no longer conceived of as arranged in a vertical hierarchy, but on a horizontal line broken in the middle. There is a dichotomy between women and men, which is most apparent where their gender is most distinct: in, therefore, their sexual organs and their sexual behaviour.

Sources from the world of antiquity and literary sources (especially in the period from the fourteenth to the sixteenth century) offer countless variations on the theme of woman as the insatiable being whose unrestricted sexual lust threatens both individual men and the whole social order. This notion was subverted by medicine and obstetrics, which supposed that a female and a male orgasm were necessary for conception.

From the end of the seventeenth century, the idea of the sexually eager and libidinous woman gave way to that of the passive woman uninterested in sex and virtuous without great effort, because she finds sexual behaviour primitive and repellent anyway. We are left with figures like the Swiss minister's wife interviewed by the sociologist Robert Michels at the beginning of the twentieth century. She referred to her exceptionally happy marriage, yet simultaneously put on record that she didn't 'really care about sex. It's just annoying that I can't knit socks at the same time.'[16]

The idea of the fundamental inequality of men and women arose in the very same period as opposition to feudalistic privileges of rank and insistence on the equality of all humans as humans, at the very time when human rights originated, and along with them the notion of a universal constitution and universal government guaranteeing equal rights for all human beings. This basic inequality of male and female came to be interpreted as the 'natural' distinctive difference of women.[17]

The third example is taken from biology. In 2008 it was suspected that Caster Semenya, the South African runner, was not a woman, but in 2010 her status as a woman athlete was re-confirmed by the International Association of Athletics Federations (IAAF). In addition to questions of racism and other offences against human rights, which seem relevant to this case, there was a further problem to consider: it seemed possible that the athlete could not be assigned to a specific gender in traditional unambiguous terms. Rumours abound here, but all that is now clear is that the runner has been readmitted as a woman athlete.

Unambiguous sexual identities have been a topic since the world of classical antiquity. Hermaphroditus (Aphroditus), the son of Hermes and Aphrodite, acquired a dual yet unambiguous sexual identity when he was united in one body with the nymph Salmacis. Divine characteristics were often ascribed to the 'hermaphrodites' of antiquity, whereas later they were thought of as 'monsters' or 'freaks of nature'. In 1794, Prussian common law gave them the right (with certain restrictions) to choose their own gender on reaching 18 years of age.[18] Late nineteenth-century medicine, and especially that of the first half of the twentieth century, decided that 'intersexuality' was a sickness. Right up to the present day, great pressure has been exerted to force observed diversity in new-born infants into the confines of the two-gender system. As a rule, gender-assimilative and gender-corrective operations are not matters of medical necessity or urgency, but are governed by a need for clarity and unambiguous categorization. But this need is not supported by human biology.

'Gender' is complex. As biological gender, it comprises the interplay of chromosomes, glands, external sexual organs and hormones, all in the context of psychological and social sexuality. In this respect, we have a considerable number of variants, which are no longer interpreted as 'disorders of sexual development', but as 'differences of sexual development" (DSD). Human sexuality is not definitively dualistic. It is multiform. From the viewpoint of biology, it is not a binary phenomenon but a continuum.

Whether we are considering the Fa'afafine of Samoa, the history of gender in traditional Western discourses, or the biological diversity of human sexuality, the unambiguous assurance with which we talk of 'man' and 'woman', and assign them a place in the world and appropriate virtues is explicable and understandable. Every degree by which complexity is reduced offers a certain degree of security. Thinking with critical gender categories permits and promotes a certain degree of insight into the complexity at the basis of our craving for specificity.

VI Gender theology

Theological thinking in critical gender-categories is dangerous. It relies on a comprehensive liberating practice, and fundamentally calls in question what appear to be naturally-ordained phenomena. Both of these aspects of gender theology upset established order, and are unsettling.

Is it possible nowadays to practise theology seriously and ignore the category of gender? No. That is never the case. A decisive result will be obtained by the inclusion in contemporary theology of a reflective and critical gender category that does not derive gender-specific roles and virtues from social conditions, biblical myths or exalted memories of one's own childhood. Instead, this critical gender category should focus our attention on power structures and hierarchies that claim to be ordained by nature. This will restore the question of justice to its position as the focus-point of theological practice.

We are all so to speak pregnant with our individual gender histories. We carry them with us permanently as a part of what might be termed 'original sin'. What needs to be done in this regard to promote a beneficial way of thinking and a practice appropriate to humanity and to God?

We must recall the forgotten figures of our own history: Mary

Magdalene, the first witness of the Resurrection who appeared later in pious narratives as a sexual sinner and as patron of the Magdalen homes for fallen women. Then there is Junia, whom Paul introduces to us in Romans as an outstanding apostle, and who has sometimes been assigned the unattested and hypothetical male name Junias. There is also Mary, a biblical subject, who has been made an object of pious history (for we must remember that the object of veneration is no less an object for that reason). And, of course, there is her counter-image, Eve, who with the eroticization of the narrative of the Fall since the second century BC, and the demonization of erotic content and effects, abandoned the category of primordial Mother of humankind to become the primordial Sinner of all time.

It is necessary but insufficient to recall these now obscure figures; after all, their revival cannot resolve the core problem, which is the basic structure of thought; and this basic structure is essentially linked to the image of the Deity.

In one of the last pieces she wrote before she died, which was published posthumously, Dorothee Sölle examined the situation of feminist theology and what 'was still outstanding'.[19] What was missing, she decided, was a 'theology of life', that could adumbrate the appropriate relationship between humans, and between humankind and God, on the basis of the notion of *basileia* (the eschatological reign of God).

For a long time, images of the Deity were orientated to what patriarchal thought conceived of as the highest in each instance: the king, commander, victor, judge, and father. An awareness that these were only part-truths led to their dialectical conversion, so that God appeared as servant, prisoner, defendant, pauper, and mother. But dialectics is insufficient to express true reciprocity. The images of God's maternal and paternal love for humankind are also important, though inadequate. In this case, believers are represented as children, and certain instances constantly promote this infantilism and put it to their advantage. Sölle tells us that what is required is a theology that rejects childishness and thinks and lives relations with God beyond notions such as 'active' and 'passive', 'giving and receiving life', and 'command and obedience'. 'If God is not the God of the patriarchate, but "more than that", whatever name we give her or him thereafter, the result for all of us will be a different, more consistent radicalism of the heart but also of the head.' This radicalism of head and heart recommended by Sölle, which has to do with the reciprocal dependence of the relationship

with God and relations between humans, is a task that still lies before us. Bearing this in mind, I close with two brief statements of possibility. *Perhaps,* as Tavita Maliko and Philip Culbertson from Samoa suggest, we should begin conceiving of God as Fa'afafine, as the person who inhabits the realm of the 'intermediate', and is exposed to discrimination for that very reason.
Perhaps this is a fundamental task for the monotheistic religions.

Translated by J. G. Cumming

Notes

1. Tertullian, *De cultu feminarum* I, 1.
2. *Ibid.*
3. Maria Pilar Aquino & Daisy Machado (eds), *A Reader in Latina Feminist Theology: Religion and Justice*, Austin, 2002.
4. Ada Maria Isasi-Diaz, *Mujerista Theology: A Theology for the Twenty-First Century,* Maryknoll, NY, 1996.
5. Musimbi R. A. Kanyoro, *Introducing Feminist Cultural Hermeneutics: An African Perspective*, London, 2002.
6. Elizabeth Stuart, *et al., Religion is a Queer Thing: A Guide to the Christian Faith for Lesbian, Gay, Bisexual, and Transgendered People*, Philadelphia, 1998; Ken Stone, Ken (ed.), *Queer Commentary and the Hebrew Bible*, Sheffield, 2001.
7. Elisabeth Schüssler Fiorenza, *Grenzen überschreiten: Der theoretische Anspruch feministischer Theologie: Ausgewählte Aufsätze*, Münster, 2004, p. 77.
8. Cf. Zilka Spahic-Siljak, *Secular Religion and Gender Divide*, New York, 2012 (forthcoming).
9. Cf. Cornelia Klinger & Gudrun-Axeli Knapp (eds), *ÜberKreuzungen: Fremdheit, Ungleichheit, Differenz*, Münster, 2008; Myra Marx Ferree, 'Inequality, Intersectionality and the Politics of Discourse: Framing Feminist Alliances', in Emanuela Lombardo, Petra Meier & Mieke Verloo (eds), *The Discursive Politics of Gender Equality: Stretching, Bending, Exclusion*, New York, 2010.
10. Cf. O. Brunner, *Verfassungs- und Sozialgeschichte*, Göttingen, ^{2}1968, p. 110.
11. Cf. Herb Goldberg, *The Hazards of Being Male: Surviving the Myth of Masculine Privilege*, n. p., 1987.
12. Cf. Edward O. Wilson, *Sociobiology*, Cambridge, MA, 1980; Richard Dawkins, *The Selfish Gene*, New York, 1976.
13. Cf. Philip Culbertson & Tavita Maliko, '"A Go-string is not Samoan": Exploring a Transgressive Third-Gender Pasifika Theology', in Regina Ammicht Quinn, Norbert Reck *et al* (eds), *Homosexualities*, *Concilium* 2008:1, pp. 62–72.
14. Thomas Laqueur, *Auf den Leib geschrieben: Die Inszenierung der Geschlechter von der Antike bis Freud*, Frankfurt, 1992, p. 21.
16. Robert Michels, *Die Grenze der Geschlechtermoral*, Munich & Leipzig, 1911, p. 143.
17. Cf. Andrea Maihofer, ‚Geschlecht als hegemonialer Diskurs. Ansätze zu einer kritischen Theorie des "Geschlechts"', in Theresa Wobbe & Gesa Lindemann (eds), *Denkachsen:*

Zur theoretischen und institutionellen Rede vom Geschlecht, Frankfurt am Main, 1994, pp. 236–64; 239.
18. Annette Kolbe, *Intersexualität, Zweigeschlechtlichkeit und Verfassungsrecht: Eine interdisziplinäre Untersuchung*, Baden-Baden, 2010.
19. Dorothee Sölle, 'Was erreicht ist–was noch aussteht: Einführung in die feministische Theologie', in Irene Dingel (ed.), *Feministische Theologie und Gender-Forschung: Bilanz–Perspektiven–Akzente*, Leipzig, 2003, pp. 9–22.

Gender, Politics and the Catholic Church

REBEKA JADRANKA ANIĆ

I Introduction

In 2004, the Vatican Congregation for the Doctrine of the Faith published a *Letter to the Bishops of the Catholic Church on the Collaboration of Men and Women in the Church and in the World*.[1] Its presentation of the concept of gender was entirely negative. Competition and struggle between women and men, as well as destruction of the idea of the family, were associated with gender. As a notion, it was criticized for its applicability only to men and for its dissimulation behind forms of anthropology that sought not only to liberate women from a biological dualism but, so it seemed, to promote equality between men and women, effectively call in question natural parenthood, and encourage homosexuality and polymorphous sexuality (2).

The Justice and Peace Commission of the German Bishops' Conference issued the document *Geschlechtergerechtigkeit und weltkirchliches Handeln*[2] on the just treatment of gender and the attitude of the universal Church, in which gender policies and 'gender mainstreaming' were assessed favourably. When defining the terms 'gender' and 'gender mainstreaming', the Commission followed the practice of international and EU documents. The term 'gender' was interpreted as a social and cultural aspect of difference between men and women, which was not the same as the difference between the biological sexes. The term 'gender mainstreaming' was taken to be a principle of action or a method intended to help women and men, once liberated from the traditional attribution of roles, to gain access to all areas of life. The Commission decided that 'gender mainstreaming' was an appropriate term for promoting equitable relations between men and women in the Church, and an instrument that accorded with the Church's main activity, which was to highlight injustice and structural violence and try to find approaches to and means of preventing them. The Commission stressed the scriptural and theological basis of gender-sensitive policies.

These two documents showed that the Catholic Church featured two parallel ways of understanding the concept of gender. One interpreted gender by reference to the meaning attributed to the term in international political documents, and the other followed a certain interpretation found within the Church. This article is particularly concerned with the sources of thinking about gender that have influenced the second of these attitudes. I shall cite Croatia as an example when discussing the consequences of this inner-church interpretation. To underline the differences between the two approaches, I shall give a short account of the interpretation of gender in the political context and in certain documents of the Holy See.

II The political context

The notion of gender appeared in United Nations documents for the first time during the World Conference on Population and Development held in Cairo in 1994. Nevertheless, it was not discussed at that conference. The term 'gender' became a subject of discussion during the preparations for the Fourth World Conference on Women in Beijing in 1995. The Vatican delegation and the delegations of certain Islamic countries opposed the use of the term 'gender'. The Commission on the Condition of Women, which prepared the Conference, set up an informal contact group. This group approved a declaration which held that (1) the word 'gender' should be used and understood in its ordinary sense as admitted in general usage, as well as in numerous forums and conferences of the United Nations Organization; (2) there was no reason to believe that the Platform for Action intended to use any acceptation or connotation of the word that differed from the usage accepted hitherto.[3] Although the concept of gender appeared in the Platform for Action and the meaning of 'usage accepted hitherto', the word itself was used about 200 times, usually as a mere replacement for 'men and women', as in references to 'gender equality' (that is, equality between women and men).

After the Beijing Conference, the expressions 'gender', 'gender equality', 'gender mainstreaming' and 'gender perspective' achieved general social use. In 1997, the Economic and Social Council of the UN

General Assembly (ECOSOC) provided a definition of 'gender mainstreaming' in order to introduce a 'gender perspective' into the policies and programmes of the UN structure: 'Mainstreaming a gender perspective is the process of assessing the implications for women and men of any planned action, including legislation, policies or programmes, in all areas and at all levels. It is a strategy for making women's as well as men's concerns and experiences an integral dimension of the design, implementation, monitoring and evaluation of policies and programmes in all political, economic and societal spheres so that women and men benefit from equality and inequality is not perpetuated. The ultimate goal is to achieve gender equality'.[4] The Economic and Social Council emphasized the proposition that 'gender mainstreaming' was a method of ensuring gender equality. This concept of equality did not imply that women and men should become equal in terms of identity, but that their rights, responsibilities and opportunities should not depend on their having been born men or women.[5]

This definition of 'gender mainstreaming' and the principles of implementation were included in UN regulations. In the EU context, the meaning ascribed to 'gender' was no different to that which the UN Organization attributed to the term, as can be seen in *100 Words for Equality, A Glossary of Terms on Equality between Women and Men* prepared by the European Commission Unit in Charge of Equal Opportunities.[6] This glossary could help to ensure the existence of a common understanding of the relevant terminology at a European level.

III   Statements of the Holy See

After the Fourth World Conference on Women in Beijing, the Vatican published a document entitled *Reservations and Statements of Interpretation of the Holy See* together with a *Statement of Interpretation of the Term 'gender'*. According to these declarations, the Holy See agreed that the word 'gender' should be understood in accordance with the 'common usage' of the United Nations, but also contributed its own interpretation. For the Holy See, 'gender' was based on biological sexual identity, male or female.[7] The Holy See referred to the Platform for Action, which clearly mentioned 'two sexes' and 'excluded ambiguous interpretations based on visions of the world according to which sexual identity could be adapted to new and different ends'.[8] Although the Vatican conceived of the term 'gender' as based essentially on biological sexual identity, it distanced itself from a 'biological determinist vision which understood all roles and relations between the two sexes as fixed in a single static form'.[9]

The Holy See repeated this understanding of the concept of gender in other declarations. Representatives of the Holy See assessed UN Women, the United Nations Entity for Gender Equality and the Empowerment of Women (created by the General Assembly in 2010), in accordance with Catholic social teaching.[10] On this occasion, they re-emphasized the point that the Holy See's priority was always to understand gender as something 'based on the biological sexual identity of men and women', and that the term 'gender' was a critical instance for the Catholic Church only when a certain lobby sought to propagate an extreme 'gender ideology' that was wholly indifferent to the fact that humans were born men or women.[11]

These declarations showed that the Holy See accepted the term 'gender', but wished it to remain in the context of heterosexual relations, all the more because it was irremediably linked to biological sex. The Holy See's interpretation of gender did not allow 'gender mainstreaming' to be understood in terms of equality between men and women, but only in terms of an assurance that the concept of gender would not make it possible to include the rights of homosexual men and women ('transgendered' in the general sense of individuals who did not accept the gender role ascribed to them at birth) in legislation. When pronouncing on homosexuality, the Holy See used the term 'sexual orientation'.[12]

IV Church documents

Although it is the most important, the document of the Congregation for the Doctrine of the Faith, the *Letter to the Bishops of the Catholic Church on the Collaboration of Men and Women in the Church and in the World* (2004), was not the first document to criticize the idea of gender. This *Letter*'s suppositions regarding the concept of gender relied on previous documents of the Pontifical Council for the Family. With regard to the 'complex question of gender', the *Letter* referred to a single source: the document of the Pontifical Council for the Family entitled *Family, Marriage and de facto Union*.[13] Once again this Pontifical Council document cited another document of the same Pontifical Council on family rights (*The Family and Family Rights*, 1999) as its sole source of information on gender and gender ideology.[14] The footnotes to this 1999 document offer no conclusive evidence of the sources of its information on gender.

In accordance with the declarations of the Holy See, the abovementioned documents interpreted the concept of gender as acceptable only if it was based on biological identity. These documents did not even mention the interpretation of the notion of gender in international political documents. Instead, the document *The Family and Family Rights* maintained that at the Beijing Conference a theory had appeared which 'dared to introduce "gender ideology" into the culture of peoples' (n. 74). It described the main characteristic of gender ideology as its reliance on an individualist anthropology of radical neo-liberalism and Marxism, and of radical feminism, and on authors who promoted sexual freedom and the right to abortion.

What is the origin of such positions? Why do these church documents avoid the meaning of gender as an analytical category in university-level subjects, as well as the interpretations of the terms 'gender' and 'gender mainstreaming' to be found in international political documents, while focussing entirely on gender ideology? *Lexicon, Termini ambigui e discussi su famiglia, vita e questioni etiche* is very relevant here.[15] This work was approved by the Congregation for the Doctrine of the Faith and was published by the Pontifical Council for the Family. Its creation was raised originally at a meeting of non-governmental organizations in 1999. It became clear on this occasion that the various participants in UN conferences and sessions, and parliamentarians and members of the apostolic movement, ought to be 'aware of ambiguous terms and expressions' that could mislead them and were important in arriving at moral judgements.[16] The aim of the *Lexicon* was to demonstrate the 'true content and truth' of certain ambiguous or suspicious terms and, to trace 'their origin, evolution and propagation',[17] and to allow direct, analytical and clear access to various concepts.[18] The *Lexicon* cited the concept of gender as one of the terms that was found to be especially problematical.[19]

Marianne Heimbach-Steins rightly criticized the way in which the idea of gender was presented in this *Lexicon* and pointed out that the authors of the articles said nothing about scientific discussion of the category of gender and its meaning, and manufactured their own abject image of the enemy: of, that is, feminism. For the most part, the hypotheses which they attributed to gender feminists were not based on direct study of the sources but were transferred from collections of texts ascribed to gender feminists or to others. The authors completely ignored the analytical implications of gender as a category and were unaware of the important distinction between the scientific and political levels; between law and morality; and between analytical and normative ethics. They developed the scenario of a disastrous worldwide conspiracy in which gender feminists benefited from the Fourth World Conference of Women in Beijing and used it to start a new cultural revolution.[20] It is important to note that none of the *Lexicon*'s articles that mention the idea of gender departs from the postulated gender ideology, or takes the acceptation of the term in international documents into account. It is especially pertinent to register the sources of their information on gender ideology. There is a good example of this in Oscar Alzamora Revoreda's article *Ideologia di genere: pericoli e portata*.[21]

Alzamora Revoredo bases his article on *La decostruzione della donna* by the Catholic writer and activist Dale O'Leary.[22] This work had a major effect on the delegates of Catholic, conservative and fundamentalist non-governmental associations at the Fourth International Conference in Beijing.[23] O'Leary's book *Gender Agenda* (1997) amply demonstrates how she arrived at her understanding of gender ideology.[24] It shows that, even before the Beijing Conference, there was a widespread belief that the word 'gender' was a code concealing a secret plan to promote homosexual rights. The Catholic delegates who knew nothing about the meaning of the word before the Beijing Conference were given copies of the manual used for the *Re-Imagining Gender* course at Hunter College.[25] Texts which were intended to introduce students to new theories and to stimulate discussion were presented to delegates as texts used to indoctrinate students and were interpreted apart from their original theoretical context.

O'Leary linked her ideas of gender ideology with the hypotheses of the philosopher and anti-feminist Christine Hoff Sommers. O'Leary took the term 'gender feminism' (which Christina Hoff Sommers used for the first time in her 1994 book *Who Stole Feminism?*), and accepted Sommers's division of the feminist movement into several currents: the primordial, old, intellectual, just and liberal feminism, and the new form of feminism, gender feminism. The latter came into existence in the 1960s, and Sommers described it as a neo-liberal, anti-intellectual, irrational, unjust, elitist and ideological movement. Sommers proffered a definition of gender feminism based not on an analysis of feminist theory but on her own opinion that after the 1960s the feminist movement began to veer in a wrong and uncharacteristic direction. Sommers adopted Virginia Held's notion of the 'gender revolution' but rejected the feminist call for equal opportunities for women and men along with the call for 'gender war' ('war between the sexes').[26]

According to O'Leary's interpretation, the Platform for Action of the Fourth World Conference on Women used the term 'gender' as a code for abortion, life-style and homosexuality. O'Leary suggested that gender feminists were involved in a plot to spread a real social revolution throughout the world. To ensure success, they did not start open conflicts but infiltrated centres of political and social power, and hid their actual plans behind vague concepts.

Contrary to the international political documents in which the gender perspective took the actual life situations of women and men into account in order to establish more just relations, Daly O'Leary (and therefore Alzamora Revoredo) saw the aims of the gender perspective as the deconstruction of motherhood as a uniquely female vocation; the reduction of population; the promotion of sexual pleasure; the suppression of differences between women and men; an equal division of labour; and the promotion of full-time work for women, along with free contraception and legal abortion; the promotion of homosexuality and sex education courses for children to encourage them to engage in sexual experimentation; the removal of parents' rights to control their children's sex education; and the discrediting of all religious people who were against this programme.[27] Because O'Leary believed that gender perspective was a neo-Marxist interpretation of world history, which made gender and not class a basic category of repression, she termed it the 'class and sex revolution' of women against men.[28]

A comparison of the vocabulary and hypotheses about gender used by O'Leary and re-used by Alzamora Revoredo with the *Letter to the Bishops of the Catholic Church on the Collaboration of Men and Women in the Church and in the World* reveals obvious similarities between them. According to the *Letter*, the new 'tendencies' of feminism over-emphasized the subordination of women in order to introduce rivalry between the sexes and, finally, undermine monogamous heterosexual marriage, the family and the nation. It claimed that the concept of gender was represented as a means of emancipating women, whereas in fact it served to implement ideologies that promoted homosexuality and polymorphous sexuality: that is, sexual promiscuity which intended the destruction of the family and natural parenthood. The negative and non-objective representation and interpretation of gender and the debates regarding gender of American anti-feminism and Catholic fundamentalism entered ecclesiastical documents and favoured a reduction of the concept of gender to the question of sexuality and especially to the promotion of homosexuality.

V   Discussion of gender in the Catholic Church in Croatia

Feminism and feminist theology are still marginal and exotic themes in the Catholic Church in Croatia. Discussions about the 'end of feminism' are especially well received and appropriate to the basic attitude of Croatian Catholics with regard to feminism, which is something like 'Fend it off until it disappears'. Even in this context, the term 'gender' seems unstoppable. It has entered national social legislation to the extent that one has to ask what exactly it means. An authentic Catholic answer appears to be provided by a book by Gabriele Kuby,[29] a Catholic writer whose ideas depend on Dale O'Leary, Christina Hoff Sommers and a Catholic fundamentalist way of looking at things that is hostile to the modern world. This book tells us that gender has nothing to do with equality between women and men but is a code for the promotion of homosexual rights. Accordingly, the word 'gender' should be abandoned in favour of the old term 'sex'. After all, the 'Catholic Church is the sworn enemy of gender revolutionaries and all the directors, clients and associates of gender'.[30] These attitudes are supported by the *Lexicon* of the Pontifical Council for the Family and by the *Letter to the Bishops of the Catholic Church on the Collaboration of Men and Women in the Church and in the World*. Given an atmosphere of this kind, and the lack of a different kind of theological literature on gender, it is impossible to use the word 'gender' without being viewed as an enthusiast for gender ideology.

Nevertheless, it is important to note that Croatia is not the only country with this attitude. Feminist theology and gender theology suffer a similar fate in all former Communist countries in Europe.[31] The *Lexicon* of the Pontifical Council for the Family has been translated into Russian, Italian, Spanish, Portuguese, French, English, Arabic and German, and Gabriele Kuby's book has appeared in Polish, Hungarian, Italian and Croatian versions. The concept of gender available to Catholics in this environment helps to induce a profound misunderstanding of the modern world, and to create what Catholic fundamentalists long for: a sense of vulnerability and a uniform need to combat the modern world. This ensures that the narrative of understanding gender is one with that of the propagation of American Catholic fundamentalism and its notion of a culture war with Europe, especially with the former Socialist countries.

Translated by J. G. Cumming

Notes

1. Congregation for the Doctrine of the Faith, *Letter to the Bishops of the Catholic Church on the Collaboration of Men and Women in the Church and in the World* (31 May 2004), http://www.vatican.va/roman_curia/congregations/cfaith/documents/rc_con_cfaith_doc_20040731_collaboration_en.html (22 November 2010).
2. German Justice and Peace Commission, *Geschlechtergerechtigkeit und weltkirchliches Handeln: Ein Impulspapier der Deutschen Kommission Justitia et pax*, Bonn, ³2004.
3. Cf. United Nations, *Report of the Informal Contact Group on Gender* (7 July 1995) http://webcache.googleusercontent.com/search?q=cache:RIhZB7O-pn4J:www.un.org/esa/gopher-data/conf/fwcw/off/al—2.en+report+of+the+informal+contact+group+on+gender&cd=1&hl=hr&ct=clnk&gl=hr (22 October 2010).
4. E.1997.LO, par. 4. Adopted by ECOSOC 17 July 1997, http://www.unece.org/stats/gender/genpols/genpols-1.html
5. *Id.*
6. European Commission, unit in charge of equal opportunities, *100 Words for Equality, A Glossary of Terms on Equality between Women and Men* (1998), 3, http://www.eduhi.at/dl/100_words_for_equality.pdf (8 November 2010).
7. Cf. *Holy See's Final Statement at Women's Conference in Beijing*, http://www.its.caltech.edu/ (4 July 2010).
8. *Id.*
9. *Id.*
10. Cf. Angela Reddemann, 'UN Women: ein neues Organ der Vereinten Nationen zum Schutz der Frau', *ZENIT*, 30 July 2010, http://www.zenit.org/rssgerman-21183 (15 December 2011).
11. *Id.*
12. For the Holy See's reservations about homosexuality, see *Reservations and Statements of Interpretation of the Holy See* (9 and 10).
13. Cf. the papal recommendations with regard to the family in the document on *Ehe, Familie und Faktische Lebensgemeinschaften* (26 July 2000), n. 2, http://www.vatican.va/roman_curia/pontifical_councils/family/documents/rc_pc_family_doc_20001109_de-facto-unions_ge.html (12 March 2010).
14. Pontifical Council for the Family, *The Family and Human Rights*, (9 December 1999), http://www.vatican.va/roman_curia/pontifical_councils/family/documents/rc_pc_family_doc_20001115_family-human-rights_en.html (12 March 2010).
15. Pontificio consiglio per la famiglia, *Lexicon, Termini ambigui e discussi su famiglia, vita e questione etiche*, Bologna, ²2006.
16. Alfonso López Trujillo, the Preface to 'Pontificio consiglio per la famiglia', *Lexicon, op. cit*, p. xiii.
17. *Id.*, p. v.

18. Cf. Camilo Ruini, 'Presentazione alla seconda edizione italiana', in: 'Pontificio consiglio per la famiglia', *Lexicon*, p. xvii.
19. Cf. Alfonso López Trujillo, the Preface to 'Pontificio consiglio...', *op. cit.*, pp. xii–xiii.
20. Cf. Marianne Heimbach–Steins, '...nicht mehr Mann und Frau', *Sozialethische Studien zu Geschlechterverhältnis und Geschlechtergerechtigkeit*, Regensburg, 2009, pp. 284–5.
21. Oscar Alzamora Revoredo, 'Ideologia di genere: pericoli e portata', in 'Pontificio consiglio per la famiglia', *Lexicon*, pp. 545–60.
22. Cf. 'Pontificio consiglio per la famiglia', *Lexicon*, *op. cit.,* p. xix.
23. Cf. Sally Baden & Anne Marie Goetz, 'Who needs [sex] when you can have [gender]? Conflicting discourses on gender at Beijing', *Feminist Review* 56 (1997), p. 13.
24. Dale O'Leary, *The Gender Agenda*, Louisiana, 1997.
25. Obtained by someone who attended the course but apparently missed the point; cf. *id.*, p. 89.
26. Cf. Christina Hoff Sommers, *Who Stole Feminism*, New York, 1995, pp. 22–9, 33–5.
27. Cf. Dale O'Leary, *The Gender Agenda*, *op. cit.*, pp. 207–8.
28. *Id.*, p. 156.
29. Gabriele Kuby, *Die Gender Revolution. Relativismus in Aktion*, Kisslegg-Immenried, 2006.
30. *Id.*, p. 68.
31. See: Elżbieta Adamiak, Małgorzata Chrząstowska, Charlotte Methuen & Sonia Sobkowiak (eds), *Gender and Religion in Central and Eastern Europe*, Poznan, 2009.

Theology in the Context of Reciprocity and Complementarity between Men and Women

BENEDITO FERRARO

It is part of human nature that men and women should seek their reciprocity and complementarity in each other.
Fifth General Conference of Latin American and Caribbean Bishops, Aparecida, 2007 116[1]

I Introduction

Why do theology in terms of masculine and feminine, men (males) and women (females)? We know that we always do our thinking under the influence of cultural traditions. There are as many ways of talking about God as there are cultures. Since there is no one culture that is superior to another, all cultures can express the experience of the transcendent, the luminous, each in its own way. No culture can exhaust the meaning of the transcendent, the divine, and consequently all language is always reductive. We always speak out of our own social and historical situation.[2] Although theological language may seek to be universal, it will always be situated language: 'Because Christian theology is human talking about God, it is always related to an historical situation, and therefore all its assertions are culturally limited… Although God, the theme of theology, is eternal, theology in itself is, like those who express it, limited by history and time. "Though we direct our thought to eternal and transcendent beings, our thought is not eternal and transcendent; though we consider the universal, the image of the universal in our thought is not a universal image." It is a finite image, limited by the temporality and particularity of our existence.'[3]

Situated socially and culturally in history as we are, when we relate to others we always do so as sexed persons. We always think from our bodies: 'Everything happens in them and from them. And our individual bodies are temporal and their vital energy is situated and dated. They are born, grow and die.'[4] The anthropocentrism – or, more properly, androcentrism –[5] that reduced humanity to the male human being had the historical effect of denying women a greater role in society and in theology. By this denial, the male human being himself made it impossible to produce a theology that expressed the full richness of humanity present in the man being and the woman being.[6] The biblical and theological tradition made us think and talk about God almost exclusively in masculine terms. The God of the biblical–theological tradition is male, patriarchal and 'kyriarchal'.[7] The application of this traditional symbolism to God 'reinforced the supposition that maleness is normative for humanity',[8] and contributed to preventing women from occupying positions of authority and also excluding female images from the symbols used for the divine.

Developing this line of argument, I want to show the importance of reciprocity and complementarity between men and women as the possibility of building new relations between human beings, and between them and nature, based on the acknowledgement of the male and female present in both men and women. I accept the dynamic of complementarity in the sense that there is a relation of interdependence between men and women. Man and woman are complementary because each has what the other needs and vice versa. As Leonardo Boff insists, 'The man possesses woman within himself, but he is a man and not a woman. The woman carries man within herself but she is not a man, she is a woman. Why is there this difference? Because what predominates in the man is maleness, although this includes within itself femaleness. In the woman what predominates is femaleness, although it includes within itself maleness, and that is why she is a woman and not a man. Having recognized this, instead of saying that man and woman are mutually incomplete, we prefer to say that they are whole and relatively complete. Each possesses everything, though not in the same proportion or in the same way. By the fact of being whole and relatively complete, each is designed for relationship and for the reciprocity that allows both to grow together and enrich each other with difference in proportion. This takes place within the boundaries of freedom and creativity that encourage all forms of relationship in all their forms of intensity.'[9]

II Anthropology and theology

The Christian view of human beings stresses the equal identity between man and woman as a result of their having been created in the image and likeness of God.
Fifth General Conference of Latin American and Caribbean Bishops, Aparecida, 2007 451

In the Christian tradition, starting with the New Testament (cf. John 1.4; Phil. 2.5–11; Heb. 1.1–4), and continuing with the Councils of Nicaea (325), Constantinople I (381), Ephesus (431) and Chalcedon (451), we encounter the affirmation of the incarnation of God in human history. The words *sarkothénta* ('became flesh') and *enanthropésanta* ('became a human being'), used to express this great mystery, show the humanity of Jesus without denying his human condition of maleness. What counts is his humanity, which is the instrument of salvation for all human beings, men and women: 'The correct translation of "The Word became flesh"– which really, because of the meaning of the last word, would be better translated "became a (human) creature" – is, exactly, "The Word came to be a (human) creature". Here we see the reason for which we said that the Word stripped himself of his divine attributes. If that was not enough, the poetic language of the prologue adds the phrase that explains the human condition the Word took on in this way: "and pitched his tent among us" (v. 14). Of all the verbs meaning "to live" the author chose the one that best captures the contingent and transitory condition of humanity, with its reference to a nomad's tent, not the stable house of the resident of a village or town. In other words, the divine essence that is revealed to us is revealed to us in history, exposed to contingency and death.'[11]

The word *anthropos* means 'human being', 'person', a member of the human race, one of us (cf. Phil 2.7). It does not deny the maleness of Jesus, but stresses his belonging to the human race. 'The Christian faith does not seek to emphasize, at least not here, the maleness of Jesus, as though this maleness had been privileged by God in the incarnation to the detriment of femininity. Jesus is a "man", a "male", only accidentally. If God had revealed himself as a human being in a different culture, he could have revealed himself as a "woman", a "female", without any change in the essence of what he wanted to reveal.'[12]

III The meaning of Jesus' humanity

He worked with human hands, he thought with a human mind. He acted with a human will, and with a human heart he loved.
Vatican II, *Gaudium et spes* 22

We believe that in Jesus' humanity we can find an assertion of the equality between men and women, in that it expresses qualities of male and female that we find displayed in his historical attitudes: 'Restore Jesus to his central position, see him live; hear, as far as this is possible, the tone of his voice, his outbursts of anger and impatience, but also his moments of affection and piety... No longer God himself visiting the earth..., but a being completely human who comes to reveal to us–precisely by being human–what there is within us that is totally other, what there is, perhaps, that is indeed divine.'[13]

When we analyse the attitudes of Jesus of Nazareth described in the gospels, we can see that his historical identity has never been a problem for the poor, black people, women and indigenous people, or for the followers of other religions (Hinduism, Buddhism, *candomblé*). To the degree that we can shake off interpretations connected with the tradition of machismo and patriarchy that see Jesus' maleness as the only path to understanding salvation, we can find another way of expressing the mystery of the presence of God in history. For this reason, the feminist approach condemns all language that stresses, among the various interpretations, the normativity and universalization of the male and relegates women's experiences to a secondary position.[14] Quite apart from its critique, feminist theology helps us to understand Jesus' humanity in all its wholeness: 'Given the affirmation that the incarnation is inclusive of the humanity of all human beings of all races and historical conditions and both genders, it becomes clear that Jesus the Christ's ability to be saviour does not reside in his maleness, but in his loving, liberating history in the midst of the powers of evil and oppression... Theology will have come of age when the particularity that is highlighted is not Jesus' historical sex but the scandal of his option for the poor and marginalized in the Spirit of his compassionate, liberating Sophia-God. That is the scandal of particularity that really matters, aimed as it is toward the creation of a new order of wholeness in justice. Towards that end, feminist theological speech about Jesus the Wisdom of God shifts the focus of reflection off maleness and onto the whole theological significance of what transpired in the Christ event.'[15]

IV Men and women in communion with other human beings, with God and with nature

In God's marvellous design, man and woman are called to live in communion with Him, in communion with each other and with all creation.
Fifth General Conference of Latin American and Caribbean Bishops, Aparecida, 2007, 470

We are committed to the building of *a different* world that is possible and increasingly *urgent*. It is the dynamic of the utopia of the Kingdom of God (*malkut Yahweh*) proclaimed by Jesus, which we seek to anticipate in the great causes that, in this age of globalization, inevitably become world issues.[16] The indigenous utopia of 'living well'–*sumak kawsay* in Quechua–asserts that: 'Living Well must combine with Living Well with Others: we are not living well if we are not living well together and, understood in its holistic sense, this means harmony among humans, harmony with the other species…and living with the whole of nature in an integral harmony.'[17] Building this new form of harmonious living requires a new alliance between men (males) and women and between both and nature, with full respect for the Community of Life.

V (Male) man liberated in woman's liberation

In Latin America and the Caribbean there is a need to overcome the attitude of "machismo" that ignores the new order represented by Christianity, in which the "equal dignity and responsibility of women in relation to men is recognized and proclaimed".
Fifth General Conference of Latin American and Caribbean Bishops, Aparecida, 2007 453

Men and women are responsible for building a healthy life along the lines indicated by 'Living well and living well together' (*sumak kawsay*). As the Fifth General Conference of Latin American and Caribbean Bishops reminds us, in the Aparecida document, we are challenged to abandon *machismo*, the vision of male supremacy and patriarchy present in our continent and, more generally, throughout the world. In women's liberation, men, males, can also find their own liberation: 'The struggle against patriarchy is not just a struggle for women, but for all human beings. Both men and women have been dehumanized by the type of relationship based on the use of power as domination of one over the other, though we must always remember that the main victims have been women, who have been treated with greater brutality. Above all, however, men, after centuries of macho patriarchal socialization, must be renewed. Today's male crisis consists precisely in the difficulty men have in integrating the feminine in themselves, after millennia of emphasis to the contrary. Certainly, they cannot be left alone in this task of self-regeneration; left to themselves, they would not be able to make the qualitative leap. Therefore the presence of women at their side is important. They can call forth in men the feminine hidden under the ash of centuries. They can be collaborators in bringing to birth a new and humanizing relationship.'[18] Paulo Freire's *Pedagogy of the Oppressed* is relevant here for its reminder that no one liberates anyone, for liberation is a communal task.

With the emancipation of women, men too will be liberated, and this liberation will have repercussions on theology, certainly making it more inclusive and democratic: 'In the light of the "irruption of women within the irruption of the poor"...it was impossible to carry on with the same patterns of thought or repeat the same theological formulations. Something very deep within human beings was beginning to be touched and awakened. Hence the necessity for a more inclusive theology, a theology able to take account of the different experiences and emphases of the mystery of God, a theology that conceives of Christology in broader and less sexist terms than hitherto.'[20]

VI Seeking communion: equal and different

The empowerment of women as a result of the process of emancipation that has taken place especially in the last few decades points to a new cultural relationship between women and men. We are invited to the adventure of building a community of people equal but different in the image of the relationships between the persons of the Trinity. These will be relations of equality, freedom and collaboration, and point towards communion, incarnating, in this new sociability, the values of mutuality, reciprocity, unity and peace.

It is obvious, however, that this work of construction will not take place automatically and without conflicts, since 'the feminist spirit on the rise since the last century has not been given recognition by traditional religious circles. Women are affirming new languages, new values and new sets of symbols. They are changing not just the understanding of anthropology and theology, but opening up spaces for human beings to live together in new ways. Traditional Christian spirituality does not realize how far women have come. There is a mutual threat. On one side, women represent a new power emerging, and on the other the churches represent the power of the patriarchal tradition that many regard as immutable. The tensions suggest surprises ahead in this difficult relationship.'[21] But hope tells us that the road, though long, holds promise for the good of humanity and nature itself. The new man and the new woman will emerge from this new relationship and it will influence the way their sons and daughters live.[22]

VII Men and women building new relationships

The relation between man and woman is one of reciprocity and mutual collaboration. This means seeking harmony and complementarity and working by combining efforts. Woman is co-responsible, with man, for the present and future of our human society.
Fifth General Conference of Latin American and Caribbean Bishops, Aparecida, 2007 452

To reach brotherly and sisterly harmony, men and women are invited to treat each other with brotherly tenderness and sisterly affection, reflecting their vocation to build a community of equals in the family, in the faith community and in society. Here again, the community of the Trinity can help us to understand the equality between men and women. 'The Trinity understood in human terms as a communion of Persons lays the foundations for a society of brothers and sisters, of equals, in which dialogue and consensus are the basic constituents of living together in both the world and the Church.'[23]

This brotherly and sisterly harmony has incalculable consequences for the collective, communal dimension: 'First, boys and girls educated in a pluralist society like this would no longer, from birth, regard as "natural" a society in which women are inferior to men, and so would not regard as "natural" a society that is hierarchical, authoritarian and unequal, for the natural state would now be a democratic, non-competitive world, based on sharing...Sharing–and not competition between men and women–would make female and male sexualities converge rather than diverge...The undeclared war waged between men and women, which is the product of a patriarchal and class-based society, would come to an end. What is more, this integration of men and women, each preserving their own particularity, could lead to a reintegration with the environment and, above all, within each boy and girl, to a reintegration of the ego with the body.'[24]

VIII   A new society based on new relationships

A new society is the product of new relationships between men who will no longer be afraid of living the female that inhabits them and women who, abandoning the values of male supremacy that they have absorbed into their lives over centuries, 'will be able to find ways of expressing the maleness so fiercely repressed for millennia, in interaction with the female that they live explicitly as women'.[24]

A new society will be achieved by overcoming the patriarchal culture 'marked by a way of living based on appropriation, suspicion, control, domination, subjection, sexual discrimination and war... The battle to defeat patriarchalism is a battle for hominization, for the recovery of our true humanity, which has been denied or distorted by the domination of men over women and of the asymmetrical and arbitrary institutions derived from this'.[25]

A new society will come through the living of participatory democracy as a universal value: 'It will result from the implementation of the values of person as relation and cooperation as solidarity. Democracy, fundamentally, means participation, the sense of right and duty and the sense of co-responsibility. Before it is a way of organizing the State, democracy is a value to be lived always and everywhere human beings come together socially: in the family, at school, in small groups, in communities, in work-related associations and civil society.'[25]

IX   By way of conclusion

The search for, and the search to envisage, a new humanity seem challenging, but we have to make a start. We have to begin with small things, small actions, but trust in the strength of the seed. There is an African proverb that says: 'Simple people, doing small things in remote places, produce extraordinary changes.' Believing in human creativity and trusting in utopia seem to be the road we must follow to ensure that man is 'more feminine, woman more masculine and together they are more human and more cosmic, each with his and her own distinctiveness, and are seen as a parable of the mystery and the site of the realization and revelation of God in our history.'[26] The challenge remains: men will have to build a new masculinity that allows them to display their feelings spontaneously (cry, show feeling, affection and tenderness), and women must be able to break with the model of male domination and patriarchy and build a new femininity that includes an active role for them in the development of a new human sociability that respects differences and equality, a communion of persons equal and different like the Trinity.

Translated by Francis McDonagh

Notes

1. CELAM, *Documento de Aparecida: Texto conclusivo da V Conferência Geral do Episcopado Latino-Americano e do Caribe*, São Paulo, 2007.
2. Cf. B. Ferraro, 'Questões contemporâneas para a teologia na perspectiva de gênero', *Gênero e Teologia*, São Paulo, 2003, p. 121.
3. O. Maduro, *O Deus dos oprimidos*, São Paulo, 1985, p. 49.
4. I. Gebara, 'Espiritualidade do respeito ao outro e à natureza, do cuidado e do diálogo, na busca da justiça e da paz', in *Curso de Verão–Ano XXV: Religiões construtoras de justiça e paz*, São Paulo, p. 103.
5. 'Experience shows us that one extremely potent obstacle to human happiness is androcentrism. This sets itself against the uprising of women, the feminist paradigm, gendered action or vision, against a healthy masculinity. We are also beginning to see that sacralized masculinity is entwined with idolatry of the market, racial injustice and political manipulation.' (D. Irarrazaval, *De baixo e de dentro: Crenças latino-americanas*, São Bernardo do Campo-SP, 2007, p. 87).
6. In this symbolic tradition and language dominated by androcentrism, there is no room for the feminine. This language about God becomes oppressive and idolatrous by basing itself exclusively on the male human being. Cf. E. A. Johnson, *She Who Is: The Mystery of God in Feminist Theological Discourse*, New York, 1994.
7. This concept (from the Greek *kyrios*, 'Lord') was developed by Elisabeth Schüssler Fiorenza at the end of the 1970s as a response to the challenge from women from poor countries and also on the basis of work in biblical studies. Cf. E. Schüssler Fiorenza, *Jesus : Miriam's Child, Sophia's Prophet: Critical Issues in Feminist Christology*, New York, 1994; London, 1995, p. 14. The author maintains that while the patriarchal policy of submission is present in many texts of the Christian scriptures, it did not originate in them, but developed in the context of the Greek city state and was mediated by Greco-Roman philosophy. The concept 'kyriarchy', coined by Schüssler Fiorenza, includes gender, ethnic and class oppression in a single term.

8. M. Grey, 'A Passion for Life and Justice: Gender and the Experience of God', *Concilium* 289 (2001/1), pp. 17–26. Cf also I. Gebara, *Rompendo o silêncio: Uma fenomenologia feminista do mal*, Petrópolis, 2000, p. 31: 'We also know that it is the (male) human being that is considered the primary or normative image of God, and that a woman is so only secondarily, because of her soul, independently of her femaleness.' Cf. also *op. cit.*, p. 165: 'Language takes the normativity and universality of the masculine as understood.'
9. R. M. Muraro & L. Boff, *Feminino e masculino: Uma nova consciência para o encontro das diferenças*, Rio de Janeiro, pp. 72–3.
10. Cf. B. Ferraro, *Encarnação: Questão de gênero?*, São Paulo, 2004, pp. 5–38.
11. J. L. Sgundo, *O homem de hoje diante de Jesus de Nazaré*, II/II, São Paulo, 1985, pp. 58–9.
12. J. Maraschin, *O espelho e a transparência: O Credo niceno-constantinopolitano e a teologia latino-americana*, Rio de Janeiro, 1989, p. 135.
13. J. Onimus, *Jésus en direct*, Paris, 1999, p. 28. The same author shows us the importance of taking Jesus' human density seriously, as the best way of enabling the faith to be accepted today: 'I dream of a creed that would be based, not on the dogmatic definitions, but on the example of the father of the "prodigal son", on the wages paid at the eleventh hour, on the forgiveness of the adulteress woman, etc. This creed would not call for a verbal and "intellectual" adherence; it would provoke a human attraction and an intense sympathy. The "incarnate Word" no longer has any impact on our minds, but the voice that demands that children should be cared for, promises happiness to the insignificant, and places love above all other values will always be heard by all people and in all times. This would be a concrete creed, and it pervades the synoptic gospels' (Onimus, *op. cit.*, p. 26).
14. 'What we find here is a universalization and idealization of an understanding of God through male experience, and precisely this is a problem for feminist analyses' (I. Gebara, *Rompendo o silêncio, op. cit.*, p. 219).
15. E. A. Johnson, *op. cit.*, p. 167. Cf. also, *op. cit.*, pp. 159–60, 166–7. See also: I. Gebara, *Rompendo o silêncio... op.cit.*: 'For critical feminist theology, the problem is not Jesus' being man, which is part of his own historical identity, but that this man continues, even today, to be proclaimed, he alone, only Son of God, Saviour and himself God. In other words, culture has insisted on the male character of salvation, without developing other possible forms, forms that are also present in our tradition. These different emphases could lead to the development of a theological construction that was more egalitarian, balanced and just.'
16. Cf P. Casaldáliga, 'Bem viver – bem conviver', *Agenda Latino-americana mundial 2012.* Goiânia-GO, 2011, p. 10.
17. J. M. Vigil, 'Visão de conjunto da "latino-americana mundial"', *Agenda Latino-americana mundial, op. cit.*, p. 8.
18. R. M. Muraro & L. Boff, *Feminino e masculino, op. cit.*, p. 281.
19. P. Freire, *Pedagogy of the Oppressed*, New York, 1970, London, 1972.
20. I. Gebara, *Rompendo o silêncio, op. cit.*, pp. 92–3.
21. I. Gebara, *Espiritualidade do respeito ao outro..., op. cit.*, p. 112.
22. R. M. Muraro & L. Boff, *Feminino e masculino, op. cit.*, pp. 245–6.
23. L. Boff, *Trinity and Society*, London & New York, 1988, p. 120.
24. R. M. Muraro & L. Boff, *Feminino e masculino, op. cit.*, pp 247–8.
25. *Ibid.*, p. 283.
26. *Ibid.*, p. 279.
27. *Ibid.*, p. 280.

The Language of Creation and Gender

LUIS CORREA LIMA

I A conflict

A few days before Christmas 2008, television and newspapers reported a surprising, even shocking, piece of news. Pope Benedict XVI, in an address to the Roman Curia, had said: 'Saving humanity from homosexual or transsexual behaviour is as important as saving the rainforests from destruction.'[1] The indignation and revulsion provoked by the story can easily be imagined. Had the Pope really said this? What was that address to the Curia about?

It was a balance of the year. Among other things, the Pope talked about faith in the Creator and the truth of creation: 'Since faith in the Creator is an essential part of the Christian creed, the Church cannot and must not limit herself to passing on to the faithful the message of salvation alone. She has a responsibility towards creation, and must also publicly assert this responsibility. In so doing, she must not only defend earth, water and air as gifts of creation belonging to all. She must also protect man from self-destruction. What is needed is something like a human ecology, correctly understood.

'If the Church speaks of the nature of the human being as man and woman, and demands that this order of creation be respected, this is not some antiquated metaphysics. What is involved here is faith in the Creator and a readiness to listen to the "language" of creation. To disregard this would be the self-destruction of man himself, and hence the destruction of God's own work.'[2]

'What is often expressed and understood by the term "gender" ultimately ends up being man's attempt at self-emancipation from creation and the Creator. Man wants to be his own master, and alone – always and

The Language of Creation and Gender

exclusively – to determine everything that concerns him. Yet in this way he lives in opposition to the truth, in opposition to the Creator Spirit.'

'Rain forests deserve indeed to be protected, but no less so does man, as a creature having an innate "message", which does not contradict our freedom, but is instead its very premiss.'

'The great scholastic theologians described marriage, understood as the life-long bond between a man and a woman, as a sacrament of creation...An integral part of the Church's proclamation must be a witness to the Creator Spirit present in nature as a whole, and, in a special way, in the human person, created in God's image.'[3]

So what Benedict XVI was talking about in this address was the language of creation and gender theory. The media report was sheer simplification and incorrect, typical of the sensationalism that shocks to get a bigger audience. This question deserves a calmer treatment, distanced from explosive headlines and furious reactions.

II The language of creation and gender theory in the Church's magisterium

With regard to the language of creation, the Church teaches that God, creating and maintaining all things through the Word, offers human beings a permanent testimony to himself in creation.[4] As the centre of divine revelation is the Christ event, we have to recognize that creation itself, the book of nature (*liber naturae*) also forms an essential part of a symphony of different voices in which the unique Word expresses itself. Creation is born of the Word and bears the indestructible stamp of the creative reason that regulates and guides it. This certainty is expressed in the psalms: 'By the word of the LORD the heavens were made, and all their host by the breath of his mouth' (Ps. 33.6).

'It is necessary to go beyond the reductive attitude to nature encouraged by the dominant technological culture in order to rediscover the moral message nature bears as a work of the Logos.'[5]

'The book of nature is one and indivisible: it takes in not only the environment but also life, sexuality, marriage, the family, social relations: in a word, integral human development.'[6]

'Human beings have received 'precious gifts...from the Creator: the value of our body, the gift of reason, freedom and conscience. Here too we discover what the philosophical tradition calls "the natural law". In effect, "every human being who comes to consciousness and to responsibility has the experience of an inner call to do good" and thus to avoid evil...This principle is the basis of all the other precepts of the natural law. Listening to the word of God leads us first and foremost to value the need to live in accordance with this law "written on human hearts" (cf. Rom 2.15; 7.23). Jesus Christ then gives mankind the new law, the law of the Gospel, which takes up and eminently fulfils the natural law, setting us free from the law of sin, as a result of which, as St Paul says, "I can will what is right, but I cannot do it" (Rom 7.18). It likewise enables men and women, through grace, to share in the divine life and to overcome their selfishness.'

As regards gender theory, according to the Congregation for the Doctrine of the Faith, it has its origin in the attempt 'to avoid the domination of one sex or the other': 'Their differences tend to be denied, viewed as mere effects of historical and cultural conditioning. In this perspective, physical difference, termed sex, is minimized, while the purely cultural element, termed gender, is emphasized to the maximum and held to be primary. The obscuring of the difference or duality of the sexes has enormous consequences on a variety of levels. This theory of the human person...has in reality inspired ideologies which, for example, call into question the family, in its natural two-parent structure of mother and father, and make homosexuality and heterosexuality virtually equivalent, in a new model of polymorphous sexuality. While the immediate roots of this second tendency are found in the context of reflection on women's roles, its deeper motivation must be sought in the human attempt to be freed from one's biological conditioning. According to this perspective, human nature in itself does not possess characteristics in an absolute manner: all persons can and ought to constitute themselves as they like, since they are free from every predetermination linked to their essential constitution.'[8]

III   Gender theory in Judith Butler

The main example of the theory of gender about which the Church's magisterium has severe reservations is, essentially, the work of the US philosopher Judith Butler.[9] For her, gender cuts across racial, class, ethnic, sexual and regional modalities of identity, which are constituted by discourse. It has become impossible to separate the notion of 'gender' from the political and cultural intersections in which it is produced and maintained. Relations of coherence and continuity are instituted between sex, gender, sexual practice and desire. Causal links or expressive bonds are established between biological sex, culturally constituted gender and the 'expression' or 'effect' of both on the manifestation of desire in sexual practice. The appearance of a permanent substance or a self with gender features is produced by the regulation of attributes according to culturally established lines of coherence. There is no gender identity underlying expressions of gender. This identity is constituted performatively through expressions regarded as its results.[11]

The view of gender as a substance has political roots. The institution of compulsory, 'natural' heterosexuality requires and regulates gender as a binary relation, in which the masculine is differentiated from the feminine through practices of heterosexual desire. The differentiation of the poles of the binary structure results in its consolidation, with the respective internal coherence of sex, gender and desire.[12] Butler proposes a revolution in these configurations and their ramifications. She asks: 'What happens to the subject and the stability of gender categories when the epistemic regime of presumptive heterosexuality is unmasked as that which produces and reifies these ostensible categories of ontology? …What is the best way to trouble the gender categories that support gender hierarchy and compulsory heterosexuality?'[13]

'The loss of gender norms would have the effect of proliferating gender configurations, destabilising substantive identity and depriving the naturalizing" narratives of compulsory heterosexuality of their central protagonists, "man" and "woman"… It has been necessary to question the construction of sex as binary, as a hierarchical binary.'[14]

Butler explains that her initial emphasis on 'denaturalization' was not so much an opposition to nature as an opposition to the invocation of nature as a way of establishing necessary limits for life organized by gender. The challenge is to find a better vocabulary for ways of living gender and sexuality that do not fit so easily into the binary norm. There is a need to utter the word in which real complexity can be recognized, in which the fear of marginalization, pathologization and violence can be definitively eliminated. Butler ventures to say that perhaps it is not so important to produce new formulations of gender, but that there is a need to build a world in which people can live and breathe within their own sexuality and their own gender.[16]

IV   Radical incompatibility?

The conflict between the language of creation and gender theory sets up an opposition between, on the one hand, those who believe in nature as the bearer of a creative reason and in the union between man and woman in matrimony as the sacrament of creation and, on the other, those who rebel against gender hierarchy and compulsory heterosexuality, and reject any ontology that gives them theoretical underpinning. Can there be any point of convergence or mutual interaction?

Some data about the history of the family, based on heterosexual union, are useful for this discussion. In ancient Rome, 'family' denoted the totality of a man's possessions, including slaves and blood relatives. In the Judaeo-Christian tradition, a woman was the property of her husband or father, just like his house, slave, ox or ass (Exod. 20.17). Marriage was an agreement between heads of family, independent of the consent of the spouses. A man could have more than one wife, like the patriarch Jacob, and her role was to produce descendants for the husband's family. If the wife was widowed and had no children, she had to marry her brother-in-law to fulfil this role. Even with the affirmation of man and woman, created in the image of God and redeemed by Christ, male supremacy is clear. The husband is the head of the wife as Christ is the head of the Church (Eph. 5.23). But marriage became monogamous.

Much later, around the twelfth century, Western Christendom introduced consent of the spouses as a necessary condition for the validity of a marriage. In colonial Brazil, the minimum age for marriage was 12 for women and 14 for men. Today this is unacceptable. The patriarchal model of the family went into decline throughout the world in the last century. In 1948, the United Nations Universal Declaration of Human Rights included the free consent of the spouses and their equality of rights in marriage. The Catholic Church, since the pontificate of John XXIII, has regarded this Declaration as a document of the utmost relevance, and values the entry of women into public life and their claim to equality with men in law and fact.[17]

According to the Church's social teaching, national legislation must respect the specific characteristics of women and promote their equal right to take part in cultural, economic, social and political life.[18] One result of this new attitude in Brazil was a Lenten education campaign by the bishops' conference in 1990 devoted to gender equality with the title *Woman and*

The Language of Creation and Gender

Man: Image of God. In other words, over time the change in the constitution of the family and the roles of its members has been very great.

With regard to so-called 'compulsory heterosexuality', in Judaeo-Christian tradition heterosexuality is the norm. Since ancient times, it has been believed that men and women were created for each other, to unite and procreate, fulfilling the command 'increase and multiply'. Relations between persons of the same sex were forbidden. Israel was supposed to be different from the other nations in various ways, including worship of the one God and the prohibition of homo-eroticism, which was regarded as an abomination (Lev. 18.22). The apostle Paul believed that this practice was the result of a divine punishment inflicted on those who worshipped creatures instead of the Creator. He punished them with an attraction for the same sex (Rom. 1.18–32). The concept of sexual orientation, presupposing essential and permanent characteristics of homosexual or heterosexual individuals, did not exist. This orientation has nothing to do with belief in one or more gods or any other religious practice.

For many centuries, relations between persons of the same sex were considered as like the sin of Sodom, the attempted rape of the guests of the patriarch Lot, which led to the destruction of the city as a divine punishment (Gen. 19). In many Western countries, the civil law classified 'sodomy' as a serious crime, punishable by the death penalty. Ecclesiastical courts tried the accused and those found guilty were handed over to the civil power. In the nineteenth century, the term 'homosexuality' was invented to replace 'sodomy', classifying the issue as one of psycho-physical deviance and moving it from the realm of religion and morality to that of biology. This deviance was no longer regarded as an abomination, but as a disease. This pathologization prevailed for many decades.

In our time, there have been important changes affecting this topic: developments in human rights, the abandonment of a literal reading of the Bible, the de-pathologization of homosexuality and the prohibition of psychotherapeutic attempts to reverse sexual orientation. The Western nations decriminalized homosexuality and even proposed at the United Nations that it should be decriminalized universally. On that occasion, the Holy See spoke against any violence against homosexual persons and called on states, including Islamic states, to end all criminal sanctions against such people. The Church believes that free sexual activity between adults should not be regarded as an offence by the civil authorities.[19] This means that these relations are not a threat to humanity. In this field too there have been great changes.

Prohibitions linked to the Christian message quite often have more impact than its positive content, which should always be good news. If it is part of the Church's teaching that homosexual acts are intrinsically disordered and contrary to natural law,[20] it also insists that no human being is simply homosexual or heterosexual. Above all, they are creatures of God and recipients of his grace, which makes them his children and heirs of eternal life. Listening to the language of creation should not ignore this fact. Cases are recognized in which the homosexual tendency is not a person's chosen option; the person has no alternative but is compelled to behave as a homosexual. In such a situation, a person has no guilt. The Church warns of the danger of generalization, but acknowledges circumstances that reduce or even remove the person's guilt.[21]

Many people today experience their own homosexuality, not as an option, but as a condition. It isn't a matter of choice or even of freeing themselves from creation, but an acceptance of their own nature. For these people, the solution is not a union with someone of the opposite sex, compulsory heterosexuality. For many centuries, and even today, the social environment has driven many people to hide their own homosexual condition in order to avoid hostility and to enter heterosexual unions. Quite often the result is a double life, with much suffering for all involved. It should be remembered that, under church law, the sacrament of matrimony in these circumstances is null and void.[22] Respect for the sacrament should lead to better information for Catholics on this point and the provision of alternatives.

Legal recognition of homosexual unions is now provided for in many countries, though not without heated debate. The Vatican vigorously opposes the equating of this form of union with that between a man and a woman, and modifications to family law that go in this direction. Nevertheless, though with reservations, it states that the rights of cohabiting homosexual persons can be recognized, with legal protection for situations of mutual interest.[23] This step, which some may regard as timid and inadequate, is very important. Without legal protection or (minimal) social recognition for same-sex unions, the social environment will continue to put pressure on homosexuals to enter into heterosexual unions to escape hostility.

V Final considerations

The divergences between the language of creation and gender theory concern bodily differences, sexual orientation, family constitution, the understanding of human nature and personal self-determination. Possibilities for reconciling these divergences can be found in the Church's recent teaching on natural law. This recognizes that there are many misunderstandings about the term that need to be overcome:

Sometimes, it conjures up the idea of a resigned and completely passive submission to the physical laws of nature, when human beings rightly seek to dominate and influence these forces for their benefit. Sometimes, it is presented as an objective fact imposed on personal conscience from outside, independent of the work of reason or subjectivity. It is suspected of introducing a form of external moral law intolerable to the dignity of free human persons. At other times, Christian theology throughout its history too easily used the concept of natural law to justify anthropological positions that subsequently turned out to be conditioned by an historical and cultural context.[24]

Today, the Church teaches that this doctrine must be presented in terms that show the personal, existential dimension of moral life more effectively. The natural law should be presented as a list of 'definitive, immutable commands' or as a pre-defined set of rules imposed *a priori* on the moral actor. It is the foundation of a universal ethic, an objective source of inspiration for a decision-making process that is pre-eminently personal.[25]

It is undeniable that at present the concept of natural law presents difficulties, in view of the abandonment of metaphysics by contemporary thought and the misunderstandings that have so heavily coloured the idea. Whether natural law is invoked or not, ethics cannot ignore the complexity of sexual issues. It is legitimate and desirable to build a world in which people can live and breathe within their own sexuality and their own gender, a world in which the fear of marginalization, pathologization and violence is eliminated once and for all. For those who believe in a Creator God and his creative reason, the world is like the one and indivisible book of nature, in which nothing lies outside this reason. If, by analogy with the book of revelation (the Bible), the world is like a book to be read and understood, this metaphor can be explored. The Bible contains many books, uses more than one language and various literary forms. It was written by many authors over the course of a millennium. Studies of the Bible have abounded over the centuries and continue. The book of nature, for its part, has its own multiplicity and complexity, 'languages' and 'literary forms'. Reading and interpreting it is a work in progress.

A correct hearing of the language of creation requires the same care demanded by a reading of natural law. We need to avoid resignation in the face of supposed physical laws, intolerable impositions and the treatment of anthropological hypotheses as facts of nature. Gender theory is still very young. The Church is founded on a two-thousand-year tradition that does not change quickly. At the same time, it is spread throughout the world and interacts with different cultures. Some of these are more sensitive to the appeal of modernity, especially in the area of sexuality, others less so. The Vatican, which has a world role, tends to be cautious about changing direction. It is understandable that it its attitude to certain issues should be defensive. On the other hand, local churches, apostolic initiatives and theological reflection can go further and create a church environment favourable to greater change in the future. We should never lose sight of the freedom of the sons and daughters of God and of Jesus' offer of a yoke that is easy and a burden that is light.

Translated by Francis McDonagh

Notes

1. For example, the newspaper *O Estado de São Paulo*, 22 December 2008. The reports were based on a Reuters story: http://uk.reuters.com/article/2008/12/22/us-pope-gays-idUKTRE4BL2FE20081222 (accessed 16 July 2012).
2. 'Address of His Holiness Benedict XVI to the Members of the Roman Curia for the Traditional Exchange of Christmas Greetings', 22 December 2008: http://www.vatican.va/holy_father/benedict_xvi/speeches/2008/december/documents/hf_ben-xvi_spe_20081222_curia-romana_en.html (accessed 16 July 2012).
3. Ibid.
4. Benedict XVI, *Post-Synodal Apostolic Exhortation 'Verbum Domini'*, 30 September 2010: http://www.vatican.va/holy_father/benedict_xvi/apost_exhortations/documents/hf_ben-xvi_exh_20100930_verbum-domini_en.html (accessed 16 July 2012).
5. International Theological Commission, 'In Search of a Universal Ethic' (2009), 78 (translated from the official Portuguese text): http://www.vatican.va/roman_curia/congregations/cfaith/cti_documents/rc_con_cfaith_doc_20090520_legge-naturale_po.html (accessed 19 July 2012).
6. Benedict XVI, Encyclical *Caritas in veritate* (2009), par. 51. http://www.vatican.va/holy_father/benedict_xvi/encyclicals/documents/hf_ben-xvi_enc_20090629_caritas-in-veritate_en.html (accessed 16 July 2012).

7. *Verbum Domini*, par. 9.
8. Congregation for the Doctrine of the Faith, *Letter to the Bishops of the Catholic Church on the Collaboration of Men and Women in the Church and in the World*, 31 May 2004: http://www.vatican.va/roman_curia/congregations/cfaith/documents/rc_con_cfaith_doc_20040731_collaboration_en.html (accessed 16 July 2012).
9. Judith Butler, *Gender Trouble: Feminism and the Subversion of Identity*, New York & London, 1990, ²1999; cf. also *Bodies that Matter: on the Discursive Limits of "Sex"*, New York & London, 1993; *Undoing Gender*, New York & London, 2004.
10. *Gender Trouble*, pp. 23, 41.
11. *Ibid.*, p. 34.
12. *Ibid.*, p. 33.
13. *Ibid.*, p. xxx.
14. *Ibid.*, pp. 200, 202.
15. Baukje Prins, Irene Costera Meijer, 'Como os corpos se tornam matéria: entrevista com Judith Butler'. *Estudos Feministas* 1, 2002, p. 157.
16. Milagros Belgrano Rawson, 'La invención de la palabra. Entrevista a Judith Butler', *La Pala* 18 November 2010: http://www.lapala.cl/2012/sobre-genero-homosexualidad-obama-y-politica-entrevista-a-judith-butler
17. John XXIII, *Pacem in terris* (1963) 41, 140; Second Vatican Council, *Gaudium et spes* (1965) 9.
18. Paul VI, Apostolic Letter *Octogesima adveniens* (1971) 13.
19. 'Difesa dei diritti e ideologia', *L'Osservatore Romano*, 20 December 2008.
20. *Catechism of the Catholic Church* 2357.
21. Congregation for the Doctrine of the Faith, *Letter to the Bishops of the Catholic Church on the Pastoral Care of Homosexual Persons (Homosexualitatis problema)*(1986) 16, 11: http://www.vatican.va/roman_curia/congregations/cfaith/documents/rc_con_cfaith_doc_19861001_homosexual-persons_en.html.
22. *Code of Canon Law* 1095, 3.
23. Congregation for the Doctrine of the Faith, *Considerations Regarding Proposals to Give Legal Recognition to Unions between Homosexual Persons* (2003) 5, 9: http://www.vatican.va/roman_curia/congregations/cfaith/documents/rc_con_cfaith_doc_20030731_homosexual-unions_en.html.
24. International Theological Commission, 'In Search of a Universal Ethic' (2009) 10 (translated from the official Portuguese text): http://www.vatican.va/roman_curia/congregations/cfaith/cti_documents/rc_con_cfaith_doc_20090520_legge-naturale_po.html (accessed 19 July 2012).
25. *Ibid.*, 59, 113.

Creation: God, Humans and the Natural World

HEATHER EATON

I Introduction

The human quest to understand has focused on creation, humans, the natural world and God. These themes have done more than arouse interest and curiosity, for beliefs about them have functioned as reference-points for comprehending existence. They have been sources of broad-spectrum meaning and of fundamental orientation for human life and civilization.

This essay explores key historical and contemporary aspects of these topics in three main sections, which include a sketch of the historically-dominant view of creation; challenges provoked by feminist analysis, the science of evolution, and threats to the ecology of planet Earth; and new explorative cutting-edge interpretations of the place of humanity in the natural world and in relation to God.

II Overview and historical sketch

The scope of creation, the demands and delights of the natural world, the role of humans in the scheme of things, and the presence or absence of a divine being have been consistent preoccupations of human beings in all cultures. Within Christian traditions, the themes of creation, nature, humanity, and God criss-cross the breadth of theologies and church practices. Each theme is distinct, yet all are interdependent in intricate ways, so that the interpretation of one affects the others. For example, judgements about creation serve to orient notions of revelation, sin and redemption.

The meanings given to creation, God, humans and the natural world are

Creation: God, Humans and the Natural World

informed by the interplay of science, scriptures, doctrines, beliefs and desires. Interpretations are affected by the metaphysics, anthropologies, theodicies and ontologies of their own times. Distinct epochs and contexts vary in terms of the influence of science, the role and power of church authorities, the political climate, and the primary directions of human intellectual curiosity. Interpretations of creation, humans, nature, and God intersect in each unique environment and form axial lines of a Christian world-view. A brief historical outline will help to illustrate this point.

There is a long trajectory of deliberations about why and how God created the world. The classic Christian doctrine of creation, established within the early centuries, was that of *creatio ex nihilo* (creation from nothing), according to which God freely created everything in form and being out of absolutely nothing.[1] Beyond this central doctrine, there is a vast array of unresolved issues, such as God's purpose in creating, the meaning of God's freedom, the possibility of divine self-emptying (*kenosis*), whether and how God is present to, or continues to influence, the structures and processes of creation, and whether God suffers with or because of creation. There are ongoing debates about eternity and temporality, divine and natural law, natural and supernatural dimensions, *imago Dei* (the image of God), the Fall, salvation, divine action, providence, and a host of other topics related to creation, nature, humanity and God. Until recently, a speculative approach has governed these inquiries.

A fundamental debate concerns the meaning of creation itself. In general, interpretations in this respect have followed two main paths. The more travelled path follows the limits, imperfections or sinfulness of 'creatures', and associates the doctrine of creation with discussions about evil, suffering, death and 'the Fall'. The diverse doctrines of the Fall share an understanding that creation is not as God intended it because of the free action or fallen nature of intelligent creatures: that is, of angels and human beings. Damage to the cosmos has most often been attributed to human disobedience, freedom or wilful ignorance, which are often construed theologically as original sin. Women have often been characterized as the main sources and primary continuing vehicles of sin because of their natural inferiorities, moral frailty, bodiliness, and sexuality. This characterization makes women little more than 'the devil's gateway,' as Tertullian put it. Within this interpretation, the image of the divine is obscured or imperceptible in creation. Salvation means to be saved from this corrupt creation, including mortality and the failings of the body. Humans will be saved to a transhistorical reality in which they will be redeemed, healed and (re)united with God in an 'after-life'. It is important to understand that in this view life and existence as we know them are inadequate or flawed, and thus unacceptable. This, concisely stated, is the dominant stance within most Christian theologies, past and present.

A second path to understanding creation finds it to be truly good, even if imperfect or incomplete. Influential thinkers such as Hildegard of Bingen and Thomas Aquinas studied the cosmological and earth sciences of their day, and found creation to be good. They saw human life and all existence as worthy in themselves, and God as present within them. The natural world was a place of divine revelation, and at times occupied a primary position alongside other sources. Those now known for their 'creation spiritualities', such as Meister Eckhart, Francis of Assisi and Julian of Norwich, oriented their theologies in accordance with revelations of the divine in the natural world.

This path was never well travelled, and eventually offered divergent ideas of ontological goodness, the causes and forms of sin, the necessity and manner of salvation, and the plausibility, even from a theological perspective, of an after-life.

A key point of divergence between the two interpretations of creation, especially in their modern forms, is the authority attributable to scientific understandings of the natural world. Galileo and Copernicus, for instance, revealed a heliocentric rather than geocentric universe. This notion met with great theological resistance for centuries. At present, certain theological worlds are disturbed by the evidence of evolution. Historically, disputes about the role and findings of science have diverted theological concerns from cosmology and the earth sciences as valid sources for understanding creation. The result has been an intensified focus on humanity, sin, divinely-mandated social orders, and other-worldly salvation. Doctrinal debates with ensuing theological and ecclesial rifts led to theological and ecclesial divisions during and after the Reformation. The fissure between science and theology enlarged that between supernatural and natural, sacred and profane, heaven and earth, eternal and temporal, culture and nature, and spiritual and material. These contrasts have had a considerable effect on corresponding theological beliefs, and significantly influence the ways in which societies, and even civilizations, respond to human life and the entire natural world.

It is crucially important to realize the extent of the anti-worldly or other-worldly emphasis embedded in Christian theologies. The twentieth century inherited many theological theories incorporating negative assessments of the nature and value of historical existence and human embodiment. The boundary between science and theology became more substantial over time. In addition, the voices of women were largely absent for the first 20 centuries of Christian writing, so that the resulting space was dominated by male theological hypotheses regarding the greater affinity of women with nature as opposed to culture and its higher intellectual expressions. Eventually, however, all this changed dramatically within a few decades, and the central meanings of creation, God, humanity and nature were altered. The ecological crisis has amplified these changes. At present, a stimulating renewal of thinking about the themes of this article is producing a significant upheaval in theology and revitalizing it.

III   Contemporary trends: science, feminism, ecology

Three major events have influenced theological activities in relation to the themes of this article. First, expanding knowledge in physics, cosmology and the earth sciences has acted as a catalyst for theological reconsideration of the natural world. Thomas Berry is the leading thinker in this area, and countless others have integrated his insights into theology.[2] Second, the twentieth century saw the establishment of a global women's movement. Women moved effectively if unevenly into social, political, economic and intellectual spheres. Third, the escalating ecological crisis is provoking a massive theological evaluation that is acute, challenging and arduous. Substantial theological exchanges occur with regard to the historical succession, methods and claims of each of these developments. Work at the intersection of feminism, science and ecology makes it possible to assess their significance.

IV   Feminism, gender, science and ecological crises

The emergence of gender as an analytical category, and the colossal contributions of feminist scholarship, have led to a change of awareness. All realms of Christianity, leadership, structures, processes, intellectual methods, content, pedagogy, formation, rituals and so on, have been altered.

Virtually all theological proposals from critics of gender binaries and hierarchies touch on creation, God, and nature, from early ventures into feminist theology and biblical studies, to contemporary contextual, postmodern, and post-colonial hermeneutics. This is evident in the efforts of feminist historians, liberation theologians, and those working under the umbrella of ecofeminism.

Ecofeminism is a specific discourse and mode of interpretation, but also a point of intersection of many debates about women, feminism, religion and ecology. An early link between ecofeminism and theology came from feminist critical analyses of Euro-Western cultural history and heritage which exposed the hierarchical dualisms within this Christian world-view.[3] A frequent target has been the connection between the supposed defectiveness of creation ('nature') and the inferiority of women. The role of Christianity in the dual subjugation of women and the natural world is evident, although not straightforward. Christian imagery and beliefs about God, creation, and the natural world have been profoundly affected by the intertwined oppressions of women and nature, which have influenced Euro-Western cultural practices explicitly or implicitly. When the operative valuation of creation shifts from defective to wholesome, the natural world becomes a source for theology, and when priorities move from a supernatural world to this world, new theologies become possible.

Feminist scholars have challenged the image of God as radically other than and removed from the Earth. They attempt to dissolve or bridge the hierarchical dualisms embedded in and plaguing theological discourses, and thereby encourage an extensive change of world-view and a new theology (not doctrine) of creation. Over the past 20 years, many feminists have proposed alternative images of God as embedded in and intimately related to the Earth. The image of God as immanent, within and among us, sustaining and creating all life in an ever-present dynamic of new possibilities, opens up the religious imagination.[4] Some ecofeminist theologians are reinterpreting central doctrines along these lines.

Ivone Gebara, for example, has re-examined the Trinity. She has grounded images of God, Spirit and Jesus Christ in notions of an earth community.[5] The implications are decisive. The image of God as active, present and moving through all Earth's processes, all life, and all history changes our response to the world seen as God's creation. Grace Jantzen and Sallie McFague have explored the image of the world or Earth as God's body. Rosemary Radford Ruether has proposed a relationship between Gaia science, God and a new covenant with Earth. Anne Primavesi, using deep ecology and biblical narratives of creation, has offered an ecological theology aptly entitled *From Apocalypse to Genesis*.[6] In each case, the primary partners in dialogue are earth sciences and feminist analyses, drawing secondarily on biblical or systematic theology, as well as ethics.

Other scholars work from liberationist methodologies, scrutinizing the relationships between ecological stress and economics, politics, and theology. Mary Grey, Lois Lorentzen and I have studied globalization and ecofeminism in different cultures, contexts and religions.[7] Mary Judith Ress has demonstrated the breadth of ecofeminism in Latin American liberation theologies.[8] Ursula King and Rosemary Radford Ruether have studied various intersections between ecology, feminism, ethics, spirituality and many religions.

These contributions have challenged cherished ideas and commitments within classical Christian world-views, and have helped to advance a massive theological renewal. The rise of post-modern epistemologies, liberation movements, contextual theologies, multi-religious awareness and global inter-connections has interacted with the explosion of scientific knowledge and the ecological crisis to prompt major intellectual innovations.

V At the cutting edge

The cutting-edge revisioning of creation, God, humanity and nature has many aspects. Work in multiple traditions confronts religious symbols, the religious imagination, and religious epistemologies with radical pluralism. Another spearhead consists of incisive challenges to the entrenched and ubiquitous anthropocentrism that permeates Euro-Western world-views and reaches into almost all spheres of theology. Even scholars working on theologies of creation or nature have often maintained forms of anthropocentrism that are now subject to severe criticism.

Four specific new fronts in theology are those of the diversification of the feminist movement, the reconceptualization of salvation, the connection of creation with evolution, and responses to the growing ecological crisis.

1 First front: a new version of the women's/feminist movement

The insistence that women gain equity and autonomy has reverberated globally. There are various, even in certain respects dissimilar, women's micro-movements around the world using ethics as their main leverage. Seen in a very broad perspective, this 'movement' is a planetary change in human awareness of women's and men's equality, dignity, and rights, and signals a massive transformation of human social structures, ideologies and symbolic systems.

The women's movement is arguably the largest shift in human awareness since the Neolithic revolution and the emergence of symbolic consciousness. Viewed thus, feminism is not only an ethical claim or political movement but a change in reference-points of symbolic and social organization leading to a radically new perception of human capacity, differentiation, and complexity.

Patriarchy has been the ruling social, ideological and symbolic form of organization virtually everywhere for 5000 to 10,000 years, but now a new understanding of humanity is emerging. It offers an amplified, intensified and strengthened appreciation of humanity, genuinely including women and men.

We tend to underestimate what is occurring as a result of the global movement towards women's equality. On the one hand, theorists are engaged and compelled by the specifics of contextual contestations of gender, particular widespread forms of suffering, complex ethical dilemmas in their own contexts, protests against specific forms of gender essentialism, and diversities in women's experiences. Yet the most significant and potent overall development is that women, in all our diversity and complexity, are entering human consciousness as full planetary participants. The consequences are an expansion and an enhancement of the subjectivity, diversity and elegance of humankind as a species.

2 Second front: salvation

Salvation is a topic which Christians have to consider very seriously. How are the concepts of the Fall, sin and redemption meaningful and intelligible today? Do we still believe that humans are ontologically superior to the rest of the earth community? That we must be saved from nature? That our true destiny is elsewhere? Few people, including women, tackle these questions with the depth and new thinking which they deserve; or at least they do not do so publicly.

Evolutionary sciences reveal the continuity of dynamics, processes and patterns among all the Earth's inhabitants. Moreover, Earth is in continuity with wider processes in the cosmos. A theological shift is taking place to the proposition that divine presence is more appropriately conceived of as not only immanent, but as 'everywhere' rather than 'elsewhere'. If we no longer need to be redeemed from creation, then why is there salvation and for whom is it intended? Is our ultimate destiny in this world rather than beyond it?

Ivone Gebara offers a unique reflection on salvation and sin. At the basis of domination is a flight from life's provisos: vulnerability, finitude and mortality. The primal sin is to negate these conditions of life, which results in escapist spiritualities, a refusal to accept the sufferings and limits of life, and a fall into domination: of land, animals and peoples.[9] This flight has created distortions throughout theological systems. For Gebara, our salvation is to be found by returning to our embodied selves, refusing escapism and domination, and embracing with joy and sorrow the genuine limitations, richness and struggles of life in community and of human solidarity with all life. Death is an inherent part of human, indeed of all, reality, and not that from which we are to be saved.

Gebara proposes a Christology in which Jesus is a salvific figure, prophet, model and paradigm. Her Jesus is unique but not exclusive, one among many who calls the human community back to authenticity. Her understanding of sin, redemption, revelation, creation, nature, humanity and the divine is a new scaffold for theology. Her proposal leaves room for deep interreligious respect, supports liberation theologies, disputes other-worldly after-life theologies, defies hierarchy and opposes christo-fascism. All these features of her approach challenge and even confront classical Christology and established theological systems.

We should abandon beliefs about the resurrection, eternity and the afterlife. That would sharpen our appreciation of existence as given: ours and that of the entire earth community. It could heighten our awareness of an indwelling divine or sacred presence, a *milieu divin* (or divine environment) as proposed by Teilhard de Chardin, and one in which we live and have our being. Perhaps that would be enough salvation for a lifetime.

3 Third front: creation and evolution

Over the past 20 years, 'creation' has come to mean the 13.7 billion years process of the universe, from the original fireball to its present condition.[10] Countless theologians, women and men, have learned how the cosmological and evolutionary sciences explain 'creation'. Creation stories have been exhumed and studied, with myriad debates about Genesis versus science, narratives versus meta-narratives, faith versus scientific data, and justice versus earth-based spiritualities.

Although theologies of creation are increasing in number, few theologians study evolution in depth. Taking evolution seriously dislocates all the topics of this essay: creation, God, humanity and the natural world. Consideration of evolution invites attentiveness to processes of emergence, complexity, diversity, patterns, ingenuity and inter-relationships. Evolution exposes an absolute dependence on the natural world. We are not *the* reference-point. Earth is not our context; it is our source, affirming that humanity belongs here, in the natural world, embedded in creation. The Earth is our origin, and probably our destiny. Humanity, along with the entire natural world, is an emergent process of a spectacularly creative and ingenious evolutionary reality. Evolution strengthens rather than diminishes the importance of religious consciousness, but requires concentrated theological rethinking.[11]

In some quarters, *creatio ex nihilo* continues as a discussion topic, renegotiated with other classical doctrines in the light of new cosmological sciences.[12] In other circles, there is a more complete renewal of the themes of fall, creation, sin, redemption, forgiveness and humanity as a new creation in Christ.[13] Feminist scholarship is part of this mix, and gender is often an integrated rather than a separate topic.

4 Fourth front: contexts and specifics

When infused with science, a theology of creation affords new insights and knowledge, in particular of the severity of the ecological crisis. Creation is suffering. Think of a sixth extinction period with planetary systems (oceans, climate, fresh water and top soil) in crisis, and toxins and pollutants damaging living creatures' endocrine systems and DNA. From an ecological stance, creation is strained. From a social stance, the list of eco-injustices is lengthy: poverty and land, water and food shortages;

environmental racism; and a host of specific troubles for women. Here we have an emerging spearhead of new work on specific issues where a gender focus is relevant: climate change, water, food securities, and energy. The main concerns are human well-being, ethics and equity. Some feminists are also working from a more earth-centred view, focusing on climate change, deep ecology, animal rights, transgenic animals, energy or water policies, wilderness preservation, and so on.[14] There are many more contextual approaches and a growing amount of work on specific issues.

VI Conclusion

Creation, God, humanity and the natural world are very rich themes. They are studied from many different viewpoints, and at times, though not always, with a gender focus. Feminists examine fundamental theological concepts and religious world-views, as well as specific ethical and political issues, sometimes with an explicit and sometimes an implicit gender analysis. In this article, I have tried to describe a few currents of thought and some creative cutting-edge work on these topics, but, of course, I have only touched on certain aspects of an immense field.

Humanity is but a moment, perhaps even a glorious one, in a drama of four and one-half billion years of Earth. And Earth is but one planet, in one galaxy, within one solar system, with six million other galaxies. All this is in a universe dominated by dark matter and dark energy, within an expanding fabric of space and time, of approximately thirteen billion years, and counting…Is it plausible that the status of Christian doctrines, or of those of any religious tradition, is greater than the amazing reality of all this creation?

Notes

1. Whitney Bauman offers an excellent exposition of the history and development of *creatio ex nihilo* in *Theology, Creation, and Environmental Ethics: From Creatio Ex Nihilo to Terra Nullius*, New York, 2009. He includes the problems associated with this doctrine in an age of ecological theologies.
2. Thomas Berry, *The Dream of the Earth*, San Francisco, 1988.
3. Heather Eaton, *Introducing EcoFeminist Theologies*, New York, 2005.
4. See for example Diann Neu, *Return Blessings: Ecofeminist Liturgies Renewing the Earth,* Cleveland, 2002.
5. Ivone Gebara, *Longing for Running Water: Ecofeminism and Liberation*, Minneapolis, 1999.
6. Grace Jantzen, *God's World, God's Body*, Philadelphia, 1984; Sallie McFague, *The Body*

of God: An Ecological Theology, Minneapolis, 1993; Rosemary Radford Ruether, *Gaia and God: An Ecofeminist Theology of Earth Healing*, San Francisco, 1992; and Anne Primavesi, *From Apocalypse to Genesis: Ecology, Feminism, and Christianity*, Minneapolis, 1991.
7. Mary Grey, *Sacred Longings: Ecofeminist Theology and Globalization*, Minneapolis, 2004; Heather Eaton & Lois Ann Lorentzen (eds), *Ecofeminism and Globalization: Exploring Culture, Context, and Religion*, Lanham, 2003.
8. Mary Judith Ress, *Ecofeminism in Latin America*, Maryknoll, NY, 2006.
9. Cited in Rosemary Radford Ruether, 'Ecofeminism: The Challenge to Theology,' in Dieter T. Hessel & Rosemary Radford Ruether (eds), *Christianity and Ecology: Seeking the Well-being of Earth and Humans*, Cambridge, MA, 2000, p. 105.
10. Many thinkers from Pierre Teilhard de Chardin and Alfred N. Whitehead down to and including present-day commentators have tried to integrate cosmological and earth sciences with theology. There are numerous current attempts to relate them in all Christian traditions.
11. Heather Eaton, 'The Revolution of Evolution', *Worldviews: Environment, Culture, Religion* 11:1 (2007), pp. 6–31.
12. See for example Christopher Southgate, *The Groaning of Creation*, Louisville, 2008.
13. See Ernst Conradie (ed.), *Creation and Salvation: A Mosaic of Selected Classic Christian Theologies*, vol. 1, Münster, 2010; *id.*, *Creation and Salvation: A Medley of Essays on Recent Theological Movements*, vol. 2, Münster, 2012.
14. Sallie McFague, *A New Climate for Theology: God, the World, and Global Warming*, Minneapolis, 2008; Heather Eaton, 'Subjectivity and Suffering: Transgenic Animals, Christianity, and the Need to Re-evaluate', in *Worldviews: Global Religions, Culture and Ecology* 14:1 (2010), pp. 26–57; *id.*, 'The Ethics of Gender and Globalization: Military Madness and Ecological Stress', *Political Theology* 10:4 (2009), pp. 671–84; Maynard Kaufman, *Adapting to the End of Oil: Toward an Earth-Centered Spirituality*, Bloomington, IN, 2008.

Torah for Women, Confusing Relations and a Winged Deity
Old Testament Gender Research and the Book of Ruth

MARIE-THERES WACKER

I   Introduction

'Gender' is understood and applied in very different ways as a category or perspective in Old Testament scholarship. In this article, I shall take a short text from the Hebrew Bible, the Book of Ruth, which for four decades has constantly regained attention as a focal point of gender-specific exegesis, and use it as an example to demonstrate and try to assess the working methods of Old Testament gender research in a North-Western European context.[1]

II   Gendered Torah

The English verb 'to gender' has entered German scholarly, political and now even everyday language. To 'gender' something means to see it in terms of its gender-specific presuppositions and implications. In this sense, it is possible to maintain that the Book of Ruth tells how Naomi, the Judahite, and Ruth, the Moabite, 'gender' the Torah of Israel with the aid of the Judahite. They reinterpret prescriptions of the Pentateuch, which presuppose normal patriarchal structures, in such a way that these regulations help the two women to survive.[2]

The prescriptions in question are those about the redemption of land, 'levirate law' and 'redeemer care'. Naomi is a widow, and after the death of her husband and sons has returned from Moab to Bethlehem with her daughter-in-law Ruth. She has heard of a distant relative called Boaz ('This man is related to us; he is one of our very near kinsmen'), who should act as a 'redeemer' (cf. Ruth 2.20). The prescriptions of the third Book of the Torah (Lev. 25.23ff) require the 'redeemer' to buy the land of a family member who has fallen on hard times. This will ensure that it stays in the possession of the family. A short passage in the Book of Jeremiah (Jer. 32.6–10) tells of a similar case affecting the prophet and one of his cousins. What exactly should be done in the case of a widow like Naomi is left open in the Levitic prescriptions. Moreover, the sale of a field would certainly not provide for the long-term welfare of Naomi and her daughter-in-law, who is also a widow.

With regard to the practice (duty) of marriage with a brother-in-law, Naomi intended to return to Bethlehem on her own and explained this decision to her two daughters-in-law Orpah and Ruth by saying that she was too old to have any more sons who, when they came of age, could take the place of the dead fathers and grandfather (cf. Ruth 1.11–3). This argument is comprehensible in the light of a prescription from Book 5 of the Torah (Deut. 25.5–10). If a married man died without issue, then his brother was bound to impregnate his sister-in-law, so that she could bear a son. He would count as the dead man's son, take on his name, and take it forward. Naomi tells her daughters-in-law that she sees no possibility of invoking this law to ensure their permanent integration into their extended Judahite family. Thereupon, Orpah decides to return to her original Moabite family, but Ruth stays with Naomi. In Bethlehem, Ruth has to work as a gleaner among the sheaves behind the reapers during the barley harvest. She finds that she is looking for the precious stray grains in a strip of fields belonging to Boaz of Elimelech's family, and that Boaz appears to be the kinsman and 'redeemer' in question. One night, Naomi sends her daughter-in-law to the threshing-floor, where Boaz is winnowing barley, and Ruth tells Boaz: 'You are my next-of-kin' (Ruth 3.9). Ruth's statement prompts Boaz to marry her and thus satisfy his responsibilities as Naomi's 'redeemer'. But Boaz must first inform another family member who he discovers is the actual next-of-kin, ensure that he renounces his duty, address the elders as witnesses at the town gate (Ruth 4.1ff), and arrange the acquisition of Naomi's field (cf. Lev. 25.23ff), so that Boaz is definitely duty-bound to marry Ruth (cf. Deut. 25.5ff).

Accordingly, the Book of Ruth is a biblical text with a narrative and form of interaction between the protagonists that apply the Torah of Moses to the actual situation and needs of women, and reinterpret it to fit the circumstances. Inasmuch as the Book of Ruth may be said to 'gender' the Torah in the interests of *women*, it may be claimed to have a *feminist* thrust. In this case, gender perspective and feminist interest coincide.

III Gender research and women's culture

Feminist Old Testament scholars have found the distinction between (cultural/social) 'gender' and (natural/biological) 'sex' helpful since about the late 1980s, for it has enabled them to formulate and express their interest in textual traces of a women's culture in ancient Israel more precisely. They have been concerned both with literary forms and with genres influenced or used by women, with motifs and themes with something of a bias towards a female viewpoint, and with institutions at all levels of society in ancient Israel that relate to areas of specific concern to women at the time.

Since the Book of Ruth is clearly centred on women, debate has focused not only on whether minor genres incorporated in the text, or individual motifs, might refer to a female culture, but on the possibility that the Book of Ruth as a whole was produced by a woman[3]. The more emphatically feminist exegetes were inclined to locate the Ruth narrative in oral storytelling traditions, the more plausible the theory that it was the work of a woman author seemed. But, insofar as the emphasis was laid on the dense intertextuality of the Book of Ruth with narrative and legal traditions of, essentially, the Pentateuch, and consequently it was interpreted as an edifying scriptural composition with rabbinic elements, the suggestion of female authorship receded. This does not mean that the question of the extent to which women influenced the formation of tradition in post-exilic Israel is resolved but that it must be rephrased. But we also have to ask whether there were not men in ancient Israel whom we might, even if somewhat anachronistically, call 'pro-feminists', and who were able to assimilate the woman's viewpoint and campaign for the improvement of women's lives.[4]

This question alerts us to the possibility of a dual extension of scope that could be decisive for gender research. On the one hand, 'gender' actually concerns not only women but men, because the male sex is also influenced by the particular ambient culture. On the other hand, there is the associated point that the strict distinction between two and only two sexes with clearly defined characteristics is a restriction that fits neither what is 'naturally' given nor what is 'culturally' possible.

IV Confusing relations: a lesbian perspective

On examining the portrayal of gender relations in the Book of Ruth one is struck immediately, in the first chapter, by a transformation affecting Naomi. She leaves Bethlehem as the wife of Elimelech and as the mother of two sons; she returns as a woman who has been joined by another woman, her daughter-in-law, who cleaves to her with a solemn declaration 'before the Lord that nothing will part me from you' (Ruth 1.17). At the beginning of the narrative Naomi represents the patriarchal norm, but at the close of the first chapter a situation has arisen that is unique in the entire Hebrew Bible: a close relationship between two women. Furthermore this relationship is described in exceptional terms. Ruth 'clings' or 'cleaves' to her mother-in-law (Ruth 1.14) and implores Naomi not to urge her to go back and 'desert' her (1.16); in this, she is like a man who leaves his father and mother and 'clings' or 'attaches himself' to his wife (Gen. 2.24). By following Naomi to Bethlehem, Ruth has actually left her father and mother, a fact which Boaz later explicitly acknowledges and stresses (cf. Ruth 2.11). The allusions of the Ruth narrative to the jubilation of the first humans in paradise transpose the position of a man in relation to a woman to that of a woman in relation to a woman. Accordingly, on a textual level at least, this subverts the normative status of the heterosexual system, and there is nothing to prevent the reader, male or female, from speculating whether we should not read into this situation too a continuation of the couple's rejoicing in that 'the two become one', and also speculate about the exact sense of this union. There is similar jubilation among the women of Bethlehem when they talk of Ruth's 'devotion' or 'love' for Naomi (Ruth 4.15), and use a term which expresses loyalty in a relationship but certainly also has erotico-sexual connotations (cf. only the Song of Songs).

Even before the rise of gender research, this kind of textual impetus prompted lesbian readings of the Book of Ruth. One tendency in this respect, in the Christian or Jewish lesbian movement, is to see the relationship between two women (that is, between Ruth and Naomi) as narrated in Scripture as part of one's own faith history. The other is to leave open the historical question of women's movements, their social location and their legitimacy.[5]

V   Confusing relations: a queer perspective

At the end of the Book of Ruth, when Naomi takes the child and lays him in her own lap, the women of Bethlehem acclaim this action: 'Naomi has a son' (Ruth 4.17). They remark that the devoted Ruth, who gave birth to the boy, 'has proved better to you than seven sons'. When interpreting this verse, it is *possible* to emphasize the way in which it is centred on women', but it is also *possible* to stress the gender confusion produced in the last part of the Book of Ruth.[6] When acclaiming the birth, the women of Bethlehem use a formula with reference to Naomi, which would normally apply to the child's *father*. This places Naomi in the position of a father for the children that Ruth has borne, and, at the end of the story, Ruth leaves the position of a 'husband' for Naomi, which she assumed on the way to Bethlehem, and takes up the role of her 'wife'. Accordingly, the part played by Boaz is heavily obscured; admittedly he accepts Ruth as his wife and sleeps with her, but the expected statement that Ruth is pregnant as a result is missing (cf. 4.13). From his initial appearance in chapter 2, Boaz is portrayed with a fully male presence, but also as the one who submits to Ruth's plan to ensure the care and sustenance of the two women, and whose sexual potency is not decisive in producing the child which Ruth gives birth to. These and similar aspects of the tale help to support an interpretation that tends to subvert traditional gender references and gender roles. This was already a concern of equality feminism, but is theoretically systematized and radicalized when subjected to the particular emphasis of gender research allied with deconstruction. From this perspective, we might say that in the Book of Ruth, 'nature' is not the criterion deciding which role who assumes in the new family consisting of Naomi, Boaz, Ruth and the child. Admittedly, the actual birth of the child is linked to Ruth's biologically female body, yet paternity and maternity are not bound up with the 'natural gender' of Boaz, Naomi or Ruth, but rehandled. We close not with the happiness and good fortune of the heterosexual couple Ruth and Boaz, but with the child, which the acclamation of the women of Bethlehem declares is the token of Ruth's love for Naomi.

This family has something 'queer' about it. That is, it allows of a number of relations and gender roles.[7] This somewhat quirky (shall we say) complex of relations does indeed have a certain logic, inasmuch as it is based on family relationships. It has to do with the care and sustenance of two widows, Naomi and Ruth. Naomi contributes the strip of land, and

Ruth contributes her fertile body. Then both women as it were combine to form a single person in relation to Boaz, and the criterion is the Torah, which uses levirate marriage and land redemption to ensure the continuance of a genealogy within Israel. Once again, however, the new family escapes the confines of this logic, since Ruth, who is now a member of it, is not a descendant of an Israelite lineage, but a Moabite.

VI   Gender and ethnicity: Ruth, the Moabite

It is important to realize that Ruth and Naomi are not merely 'women' but two women differentiated because of their ethnic roots. Naomi comes from Bethlehem, and therefore from Judaea/Israel, whereas Ruth is from Moab, the neighbouring country to the East. But a considerable number of Moab texts in the Hebrew Bible represent the relationship between Israel and Moab as antagonistic. I need only cite the story of Moab's origin in the incestuous union between Lot and his eldest daughter (Gen. 19.30–8), the account of the Moabite king who tried to make his prophet Balaam put a curse on Israel (Num. 22–4), the story of the Moabite women who persuaded the men of Israel to worship the Baal of Peor (Num. 25.1ff), and the 'Moabite paragraph' of the Deuteronomic law which allowed no Moabite to become a member of the Israelite community until ten generations had passed or to marry into Israel, because Moab had refused to give the people of Israel provisions on their way through the wilderness (Deut. 23.4–7). The fact that the Book of Ruth relates the resolute love and loyalty of the Moabite woman Ruth for her Judahite mother-in-law suggests that it is more than a story about a woman, and that this tale is also used to revise the antagonistic relationship between Israel and Moab. Here is a woman who fed Israel in the form of Naomi; a woman who 'seduces' an Israelite man, yet not in order to commit incest or to worship strange gods, but to fulfil the Torah of Israel in a creative manner. The narrative of the Book of Ruth associates 'gender' and 'ethnicity' and was probably originally composed, presumably in Judaea of the Persian era, in opposition to more ethnocentric circles in Israel (cf. only Neh. 13). It is also possible that the tale is a narrative correction of the probable contemporary view that the genealogy of King David, with his Moabite great-grandmother (cf. Ruth 4.17!), was a stigma: in fact, it asserts, this Moabite forebear respected the Torah more than many people in Israel.

VII Gender perspective with a tighter post-colonial emphasis

From a perspective that allows of reading 'with' the text, the Book of Ruth can be assessed as a critical incursion into the Moab discourse of its time, and the relationship between Ruth and Naomi is to be celebrated as the biblical model of an intercultural encounter. But is Ruth really a 'model' or merely a tolerated exception? And if she is a model, surely Ruth, the Moabite, is actually disloyal to her origins and her religion, and is therefore a model of complete assimilation rather than intercultural understanding? What are we to make of the fact that in the end her child was taken from her and laid in the Judahite Naomi's 'own lap, and she became his foster-mother' (Ruth 4.16), so that he entered the ancestral line of the Judahite Boaz (4.21f)?[8]

Such questions are addressed and methodically and hermeneutically refined in post-colonial biblical criticism, which confronts gender-sensitive exegesis with new challenges. The ideologizing treatment of, especially, the theme of (ownership of) the land, and relations with other ethnic groups, is assessed on the basis of Christian-hegemonic European powers' instrumentalization of the Bible in the course of missions to, and colonization of, Southern-hemisphere countries. Then the question of power can be posed with greater precision and relevance. Readers who subject the Book of Ruth to a post-colonial analysis will advert to, for example, the dichotomous treatment of the territories of Moab and Judah. Admittedly, Moab is a fruitful country, which takes in the starving Judahite family, but the sons of the family die there in the end (Ruth 1.5), whereas new life comes to birth in Judah (4.13).[9] Moreover, the figure of Ruth becomes more controversial in a post-colonial perspective, for surely she merely parrots the discourse of the dominant culture/religion (that is of Israel), and loses her own identity in the process? Accordingly, a post-colonial reception of the Bible intent on a gender-sensitive reading will find the Moabite Orpah, who returns to her people (cf. Ruth 1.14), the more appropriate figure. Orpah's version of the events and circumstances, which the Book of Ruth presents from the viewpoint of Israel, has to be made accessible[10] (although this is possible now only through the voices of *present-day* interpreters), if we are to ensure that the boundaries between scholarly exegesis and story-telling, and between the canonical text of Scripture and its modern equivalents, are bridged creatively.

VIII The Deity of the Book of Ruth – gendered views

Intercultural and interreligious encounters are a major theme in North-Western Europe at present. At this point, I return, but with the added emphasis of post-colonial criticism, to the question of how the Book of Ruth describes contact between Moab and Judaea/Israel at a cultic-religious level in the narrower sense.

An initial observation has to do with the fruitfulness of Moabite territory in contrast to the famine in Bethlehem (Ruth 1.1). From the viewpoint of the history of religions, an underlying theme here is the concept of the God of Israel as a God who is not seen as the Lord God omnipotent but as the one who has aligned himself with a specific people in a specific territory, and in that area ensures that plants, cattle and people grow and flourish. The fruitfulness of the land of Moab is not within his 'competence'. Here there is a remaining lacuna in the text where it seems permissible to insert the assumption that the gods of Moab ensure rain and growth in their land. The Book of Ruth not only desists from any polemic against the gods of Moab, but even allows the possibility of portraying their activity as blessed and prosperous.

At all events, the Book of Ruth holds that a happy life is possible for individuals from the people of Israel only in their own territory. And here, in Judah/Bethlehem, in Yahweh's authentically blessed realm, there is little point in members of the people of Israel venerating other deities. Admittedly, here too the Book of Ruth does not exclude the possibility of other deities for groups of non-Israelite *strangers* in the country, but Ruth, the Moabite, has associated herself explicitly with the people of Israel. Her promises to Naomi, 'Your people will be my people, and your God my God,' are so to speak two sides of the same coin. The God concept of the Book of Ruth corresponds to that articulated in Micah 4.5: 'Other peoples may be loyal to their own deities, but our loyalty will be for ever to Yahweh, the Lord our God'. This concept permits a friendly coexistence of different cultures and religions and, as the history of Christianity shows, does not call for others' missionary efforts; but its extent and limits would need some revision to accord with present conditions.

The oddest metaphor for Yahweh, the God of Israel, is that of wings. Boaz welcomes Ruth as someone who, he trusts, will be 'richly repaid by Yahweh, the Lord God of Israel, under whose wings you have come for refuge' (Ruth 2.12). He uses an image which recurs several times in the

Psalms in the same formulation (cf. especially Ps 36.8; 57.2; 61.5). It characterizes the God of Israel as the protector God of his people and of every single supplicant. Yahweh's wings recall the image of a bird spreading its pinions (cf. Exod. 19.4; Deut. 32.11). In the history of religion, they are also reminiscent of the winged solar disk, which often appears on seals of the period of the monarchy in Israel but also in the Persian period and in the territory of Israel. It is a symbol of divine and royal power but not anthropomorphic, and accordingly disrupts the unilaterally male connotations of the God of Israel.

But Ruth takes up the winged metaphor and directs it against Boaz: she tells him to spread the 'skirt' or 'wings' of his cloak over her (Ruth 3.9). Ruth asks Boaz for the protection of Yahweh which she was granted, and the spreading of the cloak could signify an invitation to marry her (cf. Ezra 16.8). Boaz offers a concrete expression of Yahweh's protection of Ruth. Accordingly, Yahweh makes an appearance here, as it were in human male form, yet the only place in the Book of Ruth where Yahweh's activity is mentioned explicitly interrupts the human male cause of the birth of a son: Boaz sleeps with Ruth, but Yahweh 'causes her to conceive' (cf. Ruth 4.13). It is the Deity of Israel with power over life and death, who mediates between man and woman and thereby stands above the two sexes.

Translated by J. G. Cumming

Notes

1. I wish to thank my colleague Stephanie Feder, who is engaged in research into African interpretations of Ruth, for many enlightening discussions. Cf. her 'Judäische Mother-in-law trifft moabitische Schwiegertochter: Wenn Völker, Religionen und Generationen sich begegnen', *Schlangenbrut* 29,115 (2011), pp. 17–21.
2. Irmtraud Fischer elaborates this aspect of the Book of Ruth in the course of a wholly gender-sensitive commentary in her monograph *Rut* in the series *Herders Theologischer Kommentar zum AT*, Freiburg im Breisgau, 2002.
3. Cf. especially Fokkelien van Dijk-Hemmes, 'Ruth: A Product of Women's Culture?', in Athalya Brenner (ed.), *A Feminist Companion to Ruth*, Sheffield, 1993, pp. 134–9.
4. A justifiable question from Irmtraud Fischer, *Rut, op. cit.*, p. 94.
5. Cf. Ute Wild, 'Das Book Rut: Denn wohin du gehst, will ich gehen', in Eva-Renate Schmidt *et al.* (eds), *Feministisch gelesen*, vol. 2, Stuttgart, 1989, pp. 80–91 (Christian) and Rebecca Alpert, 'Finding Our Past: A Lesbian Interpretation of the Book of Ruth', in Judith A. Kates & Gail Twersky Reimer (eds), *Reading Ruth: Contemporary Women Reclaim a Sacred Story*, New York, 1994, pp. 91–6 (Jewish).
6. Cheryl Exum offered the initial impulse for this reading of the Book of Ruth; cf. her article 'Is This Naomi?'; in *id.*, *Plotted, Shot, and Painted: Cultural Representations of*

Biblical Women, Sheffield, 1996, pp. 129–74.
7. As developed by Mona West in 'Ruth', in Deryn Guest *et al.* (eds), *The Queer Bible Commentary*, London, 2006, pp. 190–4. See also: Karin Hügel, 'Queere Lesarten der Hebräischen Bibel: Das Book Rut und die Schöpfungsgeschichten', in Lisa Isherwood *et al.* (eds), *Wrestling With God*, *ESWTR-Journal* 18, Leuven, 2010, pp. 173–92.
8. Questions of this kind were posed as early as the commentary by Amy-Jill Levine, 'Ruth', in Carol A. Newsom & Sharon H. Ringe (eds), *The Women's Bible Commentary*, Louisville, 1992, pp. 78–84.
9. Cf. Musa Dube, 'Divining Ruth for International Relations', in *id.* (ed.), *Other Ways of Reading: African Women and the Bible*, Atlanta, 2001, pp. 179–85.
10. Cf. Musa Dube, 'The Unpublished Letters of Orpah to Ruth', in Athalya Brenner (ed.), *Ruth and Esther: A Feminist Companion to the Bible*, second series, Sheffield, 1999, pp. 145–50.

Women's Leadership in the New Testament

ELSA TAMEZ

I Introduction

Leadership by women and men in the early years of Christianity shows us the power relations between the genders. Historically, leadership by men has been stressed because they appear most often in the texts. We know them by their names and their actions. On the other hand, women appear less often and few are mentioned by name. Moreover, in some letters we find statements against their leadership (*cf.* 1 Tim. 2.11–12; 1 Cor. 14.34–5) and domestic codes putting women in a subordinate position (*cf.* Eph 5. 21–33; 1 Pet. 3.1–7). Nevertheless, there is evidence of a considerable number of women leaders at the beginning of Christianity, far more than we might imagine. But in order to assert this confidently, our reading of the Bible has to be meticulous, using 'the hermeneutics of suspicion', as we call it in Latin America, or 'the exegesis of silence', as Carla Ricci terms it.[1]

A key to a better understanding of women's leadership in the New Testament is to look at the part they played in the three distinct periods at the beginning of Christianity. This enables us to visualize them in each period and also to understand why in some of the texts women are welcomed and in others they are deliberately excluded.

Traditionally three periods have been distinguished:[2] the period covering the Jesus of Nazareth movement, which includes his ministry in Galilee and Jerusalem; the apostolic period, that is the period of expansion of the Gospel by means of the apostles until the Roman War (30–70 AD); and the sub-apostolic or post-apostolic period (70–110 AD), during which the followers of Jesus the Christ left the synagogues, founded communities and the first elements of institutionalization occurred at the end of the first century.

In this article, I shall analyze women's leadership in each period, which will give an idea of their power at a time when, for Roman culture, leadership was a task assigned only to those of the male gender.

We can read about the events of the first period in the four gospels; those of the second period in the seven authentic letters of Paul[3] and in the Acts of the Apostles; and those of the third period in the rest of the New Testament literature.

Before studying each period separately, it is important to distinguish between the events in themselves and the writings relating these events, since, with the exception of the seven authentic letters of Paul and the Q document, all the texts were written in the sub-apostolic period, around the years 68 to 110. We have no text from Jesus' time; the gospels telling the story of Jesus' life were written between the years 68 and 100 AD.

This means that when we read a book, John's gospel or the Acts of the Apostles, for example, we must remember that although they are speaking about events in Jesus' time (John) or in the apostolic period (Acts), the context in which they were written was the sub-apostolic period. This is significant, because in this third period, towards its end, there is a strong tendency to exclude women, but also women's resistance to this trend.

II   Women leaders in the Jesus of Nazareth movement period

The source for the study of this period is the gospels. In Jesus' time, there was a strong presence of women as part of the Jesus movement. The fact that few women's names are given does not necessarily indicate that there were few women leaders in the Jesus movement. That would be the conclusion of a superficial reading. Since the texts are written in male-centred language, they conceal the presence of women. This means that, as well as the importance of visualizing women when people are spoken of in generic terms (they, others, brothers, man...), we must look carefully each time the name or action of any woman is mentioned and make much of it. It means that the event concerning that particular woman or women was so relevant that the author felt obliged to include it.

If we concentrate on texts in which women have names, only the name of Mary Magdalen(e) occurs with any frequency, which points to her being an important leader. But other women are also named. In Luke 8.3, we come across two names in passing, Susanna and Joanna, as followers and collaborators on the economic level. We also have various stories about

Martha and Mary in the gospels of Luke and John (Luke 10.38–42; John 11.1–45;12.1–8). At first sight, the part played by these women in the Jesus movement is not very clear in the text, since they appear as two sisters, who entertain the Master at their house in Bethany. However, a careful reading of Luke 10.39, in which Mary's role is important as she studies at Jesus' feet, and of John 11.27, which gives Martha's confession of Jesus as the Messiah, like Peter's confession,[4] and Mary's anointing Jesus' feet in preparation for his death, makes it clear that these women were leaders of the Jesus movement.

But looking for women's names is not the best way to discover their leadership. We have to recognize that we shall find few names in this period. A better argument for the presence of many women in the Jesus movement, as pointed out by a number of biblical scholars, is the mention of these women at the end of the synoptic gospels. In these three gospels, women appear as eye-witnesses to the crucifixion, burial, resurrection and apparition of Jesus, requirements for being regarded as true apostles. Some of them are mentioned by name, but this is less important than the fact that there were many women who came with him from Galilee to Jerusalem. Mark, in the first gospel written in about the year 70, writes in 15.40–1 that there were many women who had followed Jesus and served him in Galilee and then came with him to Jerusalem.

'There were also women looking on from a distance; among them were Mary Magdalene, and Mary the mother of James the younger and of Joses, and Salome. These used to follow him (*ekolouthoun*) and served him (*diekonoun*) [NRSV: provided for him] when he was in Galilee; and there were many other women who had come up with him to Jerusalem.' Following (*akoloutheo*) and serving (*diakoneo)* are important words in the Greek theological vocabulary.[5]

It is interesting that the gospels of Matthew and Luke, written about 15 years after Mark, when domestic codes[6] had already been introduced into Christian communities, repeat Mark's statements, mentioning that there were many women followers who served Jesus, and that they had come with him from Galilee (Matt. 27.55–6; Luke 24.10). The reason why we may fail to visualize women leaders in the Gospels is the male-centred language that conceals them in all the chapters before the crucifixion. With the exception of Luke, who mentions certain women followers of Jesus in passing in 8.3, the gospels only make it clear at the end, after the reader has already read the whole book in masculine terms, of the (male) disciples.

This means that when we realize the part played by women in the Jesus movement as his followers and disciples, we have to read the whole gospel visualizing women present at every miracle, and involved in every discussion or speech by Jesus to his disciples or opponents. Moreover, we have to take into account the fact that when the gospels speak of 'the Twelve', this refers to a symbolic number, here probably alluding to the new leadership with the underlying symbol of the 12 tribes of Israel. There can be no doubt that Mary Magdalen(e) stands out among all the women. That is why she is called 'the apostle of the apostles', following Mark 16.10, where she brings the good news of the resurrection to her companions when they are sad and tearful.

In John's gospel, women leaders come more to the fore. A considerable number of verses speak about Mary Magdalen(e) (20.1–18), the sisters Martha and Mary (11.1–46; 12.1–8), the woman of Samaria (4. 1–42). These verses have deep theological significance. It is interesting to realize that John's gospel was written towards the end of the first century, when the institutionalization of the Church was beginning, together with debate against women's leadership (1 Tim 2.11–12).

III Women leaders in the apostolic period (30–70 AD)

According to Luke, after the departure of Jesus of Nazareth, the apostles – men and women – begin to fulfil his commission to be his witnesses in Jerusalem, Judaea, Samaria and outside Palestine: in Asia Minor and as far as Rome. Two writers give us data and events of this period: Paul in his seven authentic letters, and Luke in the Acts of the Apostles. Surprisingly, these texts mention a good number of women leaders.

The Acts of the Apostles, written around the year 85, basically tell the acts of Peter, the Hellenists and of Paul. But we must also read between the lines of acts that were not related, of Priscilla, Lydia, Tabitha, of the mother of John Mark, and other women, whose presence is diminished by the male-centred language and patriarchal culture. The biblical scholar Ivone Reimer Richter[7] analyzes the phenomenon of language concealing the women. She cites an excellent example in Paul's visit to Athens, where he begins his speech on the Areopagus: 'Men of Athens' (Acts 17.22 [Jerusalem]). Male and female readers will immediately take it that there were only male philosophers present. But at the end of the story we read in Acts 17.34 that there were also women there, because the text says that

'... a woman called Damaris and several others joined the apostles' movement. The fact that she is mentioned by name means that she is an important woman. But the presence of other women may be included in the phrase 'and some others'.

An important fact to take into account is the birth of Christian communities in family homes. We know that in the home, where the first Christian communities met for three centuries, women had a much more important place that in the public arena. Female citizens had no place in the town assembly (*ekklesia*), but they did in the household-*ekklesia*. There women were always present and often as leaders. Moreover, various texts speak of both men and women being imprisoned for their faith. Paul himself tells us that he gaoled both men and women (Acts 8.3), although later, when he had joined the movement, he himself was imprisoned together with women fellow mission workers (Rom. 16.7).

Acts gives various women's names, in some cases describing what they did. Two women stand out, one perhaps a widow and the other married: These are the leaders Lydia and Priscilla. Acts 16.11–40 gives considerable space to Lydia, which confirms that she was an important leader. For her part, Priscilla is a married woman. She and her husband Aquila are prominent leaders of the missionary movement. They belonged to the movement before Paul. The fact that Priscilla's name is given first shows that she was more important than her husband, at least with respect to the ministry.[8] The importance of Priscilla, (or Prisca's) leadership can be seen by noting that she appears in four writings (Rom. 16.3–5; Acts 18.2–3, 18–9, 26; 1 Cor. 16.19; 2 Tim 4.19).

Less prominence is given to Tabitha or Dorcas than to the two preceding women (Acts 9.36–41). Normally, men and women think of her as a pious seamstress. However, this story must be re-read with care, because the purpose of the text is to stress the miracle done by Peter in raising Tabitha, rather than to recount Tabitha's own life. But the text clearly says that she is a disciple (*mathetria*), who was a support to widows. Being a disciple means she was a teacher, preacher and missionary,[9] as well as a woman who helped other poor women.

In Paul's letters,[10] we find a very active female leadership. It is not by chance that Paul takes up the baptismal formula in Galatians 3.28, which speaks of equality of gender, race and class.[11] Unfortunately, because of the epistolary literary form, we do not hear anything about these women's actions, only their names in the greetings. Nevertheless, the greetings to women in Romans 16.1–16 are a valuable aid in helping us to identify the names, leadership and abundance of women, some of whom were fellow workers and became fellow prisoners. Paul greets 10 women and 18 men. He names eight of the 10 women he mentions. Mentioning women by name means that he knew them very well, and also that they were women who had made themselves known by doing something important. Three of the 10 women stand out: Phoebe, a deacon[12] and benefactor; Priscilla, a fellow worker, whom we have already encountered in Acts; and Junia, a woman apostle,[13] who shared Paul's imprisonment together with her husband Andronicus.

Of course, there were also tensions over women's leadership in this period. There was a conflict with Paul in the Corinth community (1 Cor. 14.34–5). The prophetic ministry of women was probably very strong in the Corinth community and led to difficulties with Paul.

IV Women leaders in the sub-apostolic period (70–110 AD)

As I have noted, there is a fierce debate about women's leadership in this period. We can see this both in the New Testament and in the extra-biblical writings.[14] Two New Testament texts appear at about the same time, the Gospel of John, in which women are presented in a very positive way, as leaders, teachers and evangelists; and the Pastoral Epistles 1 Timothy and Titus, in which women are forbidden to teach.

The ideology of Roman society looked askance at women who did not submit to men, especially to the *pater-familias*, the head of the household. The domestic codes we read in Aristotle were taken up by the ideology of Roman society. And although it was not always exactly what happened in practice, it was accepted as the ideal that the wife, children and slaves should submit to the *pater-familias*, who was their husband, father or master.[15] Accordingly, the domestic codes of Roman society's family ideal were starting to be introduced into the Christian communities in this period. In some letters, there is a stress on reciprocity, as in Ephesians, Colossians and 1 Peter. Although wives should be subordinate to their husbands, husbands should love their wives.

But in other biblical texts, which are harsher against women, there is no reciprocity. In 1 Timothy, the codes are scattered about, without reciprocity. Women should keep silence (2.11–12); children must merely obey (3.4); and slaves must simply serve and honour their masters (6.1–2). This letter to Timothy was written towards the end of the first century, or at the beginning of the second, and in it we find a strong tendency to institutionalization. It promotes a household governed by the domestic codes of Roman society, expecting that the Church, as God's household, would conform to these (2.14; 3.4–5).

There were also class conflicts and different theological positions within the Christian communities.[16] It was a period in which the *ekklesia* was tending to become institutionalized and to erect boundaries, limit participation and exclude people, either because of gender or because they disagreed with the leaders, who were in an advantageous position at that point. Consequently, because of this institutionalization and the patriarchal influence of Roman society, women began to be excluded from leadership in the church communities.

That tendency to exclude them continued through the centuries. There are odd data which disclose the refusal to allow the participation of women; for example, there is a Greek manuscript (Western, second century) which changes the order of the couple Pricilla and Aquila, placing Aquila first. This occurs in the passage in Acts which speaks of Pricilla and Aquila teaching Apollos (Acts 18.26). As I have already remarked, the order marks the importance of the person. The historian Justo González points out another curious related fact: 'In the fourth century one of the ancient churches in Rome was called the "Church of St Prisca"; shortly afterwards it became the "Church of Saints Prisca and Aquila", and by the seventh century it had become the "Church of Saints Aquila and Prisca".'[17] Something similar happened in the case of Damaris, the philosopher who was converted to Christianity, when she heard Paul speaking on the Areopagus. The same second-century western Greek manuscript mentions Dionysius. Later, the father of the Church John Chrysostom spoke in one of his writing of Dionysius and his wife Damaris.[18]

Nevertheless, women continued to resist being excluded. We know that women continued to be active in the orthodox Christian communities, although their visible, high-profile leadership occurred more often in Gnostic and prophetic circles.[19]

V Conclusion

There can be no doubt that women were important leaders in the very early years of Christianity. The biblical texts themselves bear witness to this, sometimes explicitly and sometimes less so. Applying the 'hermeneutics of suspicion' helps us to discern their leadership, which may have become invisible in the language used. Neither can there be any doubt that for various, especially patriarchal, reasons women's leadership caused tensions, and that women were gradually being excluded from the communities and institutionalized. Nevertheless, throughout history there have been and continue to be women distinguished by their leadership, although not as many as during the Jesus-movement period in Palestine and the time of the apostles in the Roman provinces.

Translated by Dinah Livingstone

Notes

1. *Mary Magdalen and many others: Women who Followed Jesus,* Minneapolis, 1994, p. 22.
2. Cf. Raymond E. Brown, *The Churches the Apostles left Behind*, New York, 1984.
3. 1 Thessalonians, 1 & 2 Corinthians, Galatians, Romans, Philemon and Philippians.
4. Mercedes Lopes, *Jesús y la tradición de la Sofía: Marta en la comunidad del dicípulo amado* (John 11.17–32), Latin American Biblical University degree thesis, Costa Rica, 1995; published as: *A confissão de Marta. Leitura a partir de uma ótica de género*, Sao Paulo, 1996.
5. Suzanne Tunc analyzes the technical meaning of the terms 'follow' and 'serve'. She claims that the women who followed Jesus 'answered to the definition of true disciples'. See *También las mujeres seguían a Jesús,* Santander, 1998, p. 21.
6. The domestic codes refer to household administration and command women, children and slaves to be subject to their husbands, fathers and masters respectively.
7. *Vida das mulheres na sociedade e na Igreja: Una exegese feminista de atos dos apóstolos*, Saõ Leopoldo, 1995, pp. 25f.
8. Cf. Marie Noël Keller, *Priscilla and Aquila. Paul's Co-workers in Christ Jesus*, Minneapolis, 2010.
9. Ivone Reimer Richter, *op cit.*, p. 55.
10. We need to distinguish between the genuine letters of Paul and the pseudo-epigraphic letters. The deutero-Pauline letters, such as Colossians, Ephesians, 1 and 2 Timothy and Titus, were written in the sub-apostolic period, when the apostles had already departed and we find evidence of a pressure for stability through institutionalization. Paul's authentic letters feature strong participation by women in the apostolic period. But the deutero-Pauline letters show a less favourable attitude to their leadership.
11. According to Hans Dieter Betz, the equality between the sexes mentioned in Galatians 3.28 is something entirely new; there is nothing like it either in Graeco-Latin literature or in Judaism (*Galatians,* Philadelphia, 1988, p. 97).
12. A lot of attention has been given to the fact that in the Greek the feminine title 'deacon' appears (as well as the masculine 'deacon'), which probably indicates that a ministry is in question here. According to Robert Jewett, Phoebe was probably the person who

undertook to defray the expenses of Paul's journey to Spain. The Roman recipients of his letter are to welcome her on Paul's recommendation.
13. For many years, tradition and biblical scholarship maintained that Junia was a masculine name, despite the fact that it is not found as a male name in extra-biblical contexts. However, today it has been confirmed and accepted that Junia was a woman apostle. Eldon Jay Epp, *Junia: The First Woman Apostle,* Minneapolis, 2005.
14. Second- and third-century Gnostic texts, as well as the *Acts of Tecla* and the *Gospel of Philip.* show the gender conflict. On the other hand, extra-biblical literature, such as Pliny's Letter to Trajan, describes the torture of female ministers.
15. *Cf.* Elsa Tamez, *Luchas de poder en los orígenes del Cristianismo. Un estudio de la Primera Carta a Timoteo,* Santander, 2005, p. 65.
16. *Ibid.*
17. 'Hechos'. *Comentario Bíblico Hispano,* Miami, 1992, p. 273.
18. Ivone Reimer Richter, *op. cit.,* 25.
19. *Cf.* Suzanne Tunc, *op. cit.,* pp. 121–6.

Revisiting and Reclaiming Incarnation
An Asian Woman's Christological Journey

MURIEL OREVILLO-MONTENEGRO

I Introduction

In Asia, Christologies are articulated not so much in treatises as in rituals and feasts. In the Philippines, Christology is largely associated with the icons of the *Nuestro Padre Jesus Nazareno* (Black Nazarene) carrying a cross,[1] and the *Señor Santo Niño*, the child Jesus garbed in luxuriously-beaded red satin, holding a sceptre.[2] The devotees of the Black Nazarene celebrate his feast with a long procession around Manila. They clamber up to the *carroza* to kiss him, or wipe the icon with their handkerchiefs for healing. This devotion is an expression of the longing to touch or hold Christ. In contrast, the devotees of *Señor Santo Niño* in Cebu celebrate his feasts with much fanfare and street dancing called *Sinulog*. The dancers chant *'Pit Senyor!'* to the rhythm of drums in order to invoke blessings from the child Jesus. *Sinulog*, however, has been commercialized to promote tourism, and as a platform for political ambitions. It glosses over bad memories of the effects of colonization on the land, on bodies, and on minds.

To probe the impact of these Jesus icons in the day-to-day lives of the people is in order. To ask why moral decadence is pervasive in a country where millions devotees of *Señor Santo Niño* and the Black Nazarene live is not out of place. In this article, I propose that doing Christology is a continuing journey, and that the meaning of Incarnation must be revisited to make it meaningful to Asian women.

II Looking back: discerning the nexus of Christmas and Holy Week

The Christmas season brought me melancholic emptiness for reasons I did not understand. Only much later, when I re-read the story of the Nativity in connection with Rachel's grief, did I understand the feeling. Rachel wept over the children killed by Herod's soldiers (Matt. 2.13–8). I realized the connection between Christmas and Good Friday. The biblical Rachel was the favoured wife of Jacob, and was regarded as the foremother of the Northern tribes of Israel. The prophet pictured Rachel as mourning over the children of Israel who were brought to exile in Babylon: 'A voice is heard in Ramah, lamentation and bitter weeping. Rachel is grieving for her children; she refuses to be comforted because her children are no more' (Jer. 31.15). In times of moral turmoil, Rachel cries out from her grave, giving voice to God's own anguish at the loss of her children to sinfulness. The Gospel tells us of Rachel grieving, exemplifying the pain of mothers whose babies were killed by Herod's soldiers to avert the fulfilment of the prophecy that a child born around that time would become King of the Jews (Matt. 2.18). Herod feared possible change in the order of things. Fear drove the powerful to invent ways like crucifixion to deter subversion or rebellion. Rachel's descendant Yeshua, Jesus of Nazareth, was crucified on account of accusations of insurrection and blasphemy. The story of Jesus' birth and death are inseparable segments of the Gospel story, like book-ends holding together the narratives of his life and ministry.

III Problematizing the traditional view of Incarnation

Rethinking Incarnation as central in Christology demands problematizing the concept to find fresh, relevant meaning.[3] Since language is a temporal process, the meaning of words 'will never stay quite the same from context to context',[4] and the task of rethinking is appropriate. The need to interrogate the traditional view of Incarnation arises for several reasons.

First, the concept of Incarnation was constructed centuries ago and many miles away from my contemporary context by men with patriarchal worldviews. Hence these concepts inevitably reflect their male-centred culture and language, and privilege masculine images of the divine in relation to human beings.

Second, any view of Incarnation that implicitly denigrates women and women's bodies is not authentic to the witness of the Bible and Councils that the purpose of the Incarnation is to save all human beings. Most church fathers espoused the view that woman is inferior, misbegotten, defective vis-à-vis man, and has no capacity for spiritual discernment.[5] The view that sin is associated particularly with female sexuality is especially problematic, and affects theologies of the Incarnation. Christ was human, Athanasius asserted, because he was born from a woman's body that was 'in very truth pure from intercourse of men'.[6] This hymen-virginity argument in favour of Mary's suitability to be the mother of God mystified Mary's sexuality and humanity. Gregory of Nazianzus also made Mary the proof that the Logos became flesh, but he severed Mary from her powerful Magnificat (Luke 1.46–55). Mary is portrayed as alien to the nitty-gritty of women's life experiences, reduced to a mythical virgin baby-maker or to a *ci-baji* (a 'seed receiver' or surrogate mother),[7] whose body bears a child to serve male interests and power. Ironically, this argument backfires: a woman whose humanity is mythical could only give birth to a mythical human.

Third, the notion that maleness is ontologically necessary for the Incarnation of the Logos is farfetched. The view that the Son has 'assumed manhood for our salvation',[8] even though Gregory Nazianzus warns us that 'that which is not assumed he has not healed',[9] has reinforced the androcentric view of Incarnation. Even today the maleness of Christ is invoked to argue that women cannot be ordained, because they cannot fully represent Christ.

Fourth, the story of Incarnation is told from the perspective of the people around the Mediterranean basin only. Incarnation is God's expression or revelation in human form of 'God's nature and will for our salvation'.[10] Yet, in religiously pluralistic Asian contexts, the claim that God is incarnate only in the person of Jesus of Nazareth needs rethinking. To say that one religion has the monopoly of God's revelation is implausible. If the Holy Spirit has a critical role in the Incarnation, then it might be possible to think creatively about how new bodies can incarnate God. A Christian's response to God's revelation will be determined by one's understanding of Incarnation. We discern the ways in which God is present in the world in the context of people's actual struggles for life.

IV Pioneers of dissension: undoing Christological grand narratives

Early contestations focused on the maleness of Jesus as an ontological requirement for Incarnation. Rosemary Radford Ruether asked, 'How can a male Christ save women'?[11] Even the idea that Jesus is feminist was deemed of no significance for women, because the teachings about *imitatio Christi*, as Mary Daly noted, only make women spiritualize imposed suffering.[12]

Third-World women who had experienced different forms of oppression by virtue of their gender, race and class also deconstructed traditional views of Incarnation. Delores Williams echoes Black Theology's view that Jesus is black, and that Christ becomes one with the oppressed blacks.[13] She has reflected on black women's experience of exploitation and surrogacy. Her theory is that Jesus also suffered as a surrogate for others,[14] but that his ministerial vision gives the Incarnation the meaning of creating just relationships. Christ is manifest in anyone who works for the freedom of the oppressed, especially that of the black community.

To Asian women, maleness is 'not essential but functional'.[15] Jesus accompanies them in their struggles for life's fullness. Jesus is incarnate in people who resist structural forces that steal away their life. Kwok Pui Lan's organic Christology debunks the idea that God's revelation is fixed in a 'finite, historically specific human form'.[16] Jesus appeared 'once and for all' as a prototype of humanity, a sign that God is with us. Jesus is God's epiphany but not the sole embodiment of God's revelation. Incarnation is not limited to human form. In the midst of poverty and religious plurality, Asian women see Jesus as gruel, grain, mother, and as a shaman who dances to heal wounded hearts, spirits and bodies.[17]

In queer communities, Jesus is incarnate in people who resist homophobia and 'othering'. Jesus transgresses all boundaries that limit life's possibilities. Queer theology challenges the imperial view of Incarnation that controls the 'spiritual production of meaning'[18] and suppresses the rise of subjugated knowledge by labelling it heretical. Jesus the queer loves life; he leaves the dark tomb of death to embrace life. Queering, therefore, is leaving the 'closet' of any kind, to experience resurrection and embrace life to the full. Surely, people have conceived and experienced the practical meanings of the Incarnation in many ways. Provocative new meanings dawn upon those who struggle to break free from death-dealing situations.

V The challenge to revisit Christological constructs

The nexus of the Christmas-Lenten stories moves on two trajectories. One is to re-examine what happened in Jesus' life. The other is to re-think the meaning of what happened on Good Friday. While all Gospels tell the story of Jesus' death, Matthew and Luke tell the birth story and John speaks poetically of the *Logos*, the Eternal Wisdom becoming flesh to live among humanity. These are reflections on God's presence in Jesus' life, later enshrined in the doctrine of Incarnation.

The Christmas and Lenten stories are like the inseparable *yin* and *yang* that make the Christ-story whole. These stories point to Jesus, who was flesh and blood, yet fully God. Believers are continually challenged to look at these narratives in a different light. Even as the earth continues to tremble from repeated earthquakes in my country, I write this essay in the hope that more pilgrims will take the journey to find deeper faith-meaning in their human existence.

Revisiting the doctrine of Incarnation is important for two reasons. First, the idea of Incarnation is not a monopoly of Christianity. The philosopher Hegel suggested that humanity may incarnate the divine Absolute. Other religions also believe in the revelation of the divine in an embodied this-worldly form. In Hindu tradition, an *avatara* is the Incarnation of a deity. In Krishna, the ninth Incarnation of the supreme God Vishnu came to teach believers to see the path to liberation.[19] Through Incarnation, the nature and will of the Divine becomes 'recognizable and intelligible to humans'.[20]

The women in a village recently hit by a typhoon[21] told how their neighbourhood was miraculously spared from landslides, because their neighbours were kind to a stranger. The night before the typhoon, an old woman came, to ask the neighbours to show her the way to her destination. Although the trek at night was dangerous, a neighbour couple accompanied the stranger. The old woman warned them of the impending catastrophe but assured them that they would be safe. The neighbourhood was indeed spared. The villagers interpreted that experience as a Christophany. Christ appeared and saved the neighbourhood by warning them of the coming disaster.

Second, the church Fathers' discourse on Incarnation tended to romanticize Jesus' death and the cross, an instrument of religious and state violence. They glossed over the violence of the cross in order to interpret it as the symbol of salvation. Is violence a pre-requisite for Christ's work of redemption? Is the evil manifest in the violence of the cross necessary to attain salvation? Is it indispensable to make humanity understand that Jesus, now regarded as Christ, offers hope of resurrection? Rene Girard's theory of the atonement makes Jesus a scapegoat who ends the cycle of violence by enduring violence.[22]

Violence is not necessary for redemption; instead, redemptive work demands that believers make a commitment to resist violence. Jesus' death must not be interpreted apart from his works. Jesus incarnates the abundance of God's love in his life of prophetic and redemptive deeds. The Christic ethics of Jesus threatens the powerful. His liberating praxis of resisting the corrupt values and forces of evil of his time shows the content of salvation. Salvation is made ours by the power of the resurrection. Surely, Rachel remains distressed when believers continue to romanticize the cross as the locus of salvation, rather than putting the emphasis on Jesus' entire life and his resurrection.

VI The caring community as an embodiment of the Christ

The biblical Rachel and her grief are powerful symbols for mothers across the ages, who are inconsolable when things are not right with their children. In Rachel, Jesus' birth story meets the Lenten-season story. As Christopher Morse puts it, 'In Rachel, the Gospel's link between the Nativity and Good Friday'[23] is clear. In this death-dealing world, Rachel is not placated. She provokes us to action.

Philippine society is very broken. It makes Rachel weep continuously, as wanton graft and violence are widespread. Rachel cannot be consoled in the face of massive poverty, criminality, and state violence to silence dissent, especially during the rule of the self-proclaimed former President Gloria Macapagal-Arroyo. Rachel wails over the killing of the innocents by order of modern Herods. This past Christmas and Epiphany season, Rachel wept over the death of thousands in our region due to typhoons and earthquakes whose effects were made worse by irresponsible human activity. In this broken-hearted society, many descend to heartlessness. The greedy and powerful act with impunity. Christians practise false external piety rather than live an incarnational spirituality. They do not appreciate the interconnectedness of Incarnation and the historical reality of transformed life. They manifest what Rita Nakashima Brock calls the 'alter ego of the egocentric, destructive masculine self', that 'finds no path to empower the heart'.[24] Consequently, believers do not see their complicity–passive or active–in the continuing tragedy of the cross in contemporary times. This situation indicates the failure of Christianity to impress the meaning of Incarnation on its adherents. This certainly poses a challenge to the Church's self-understanding as Christ's body. We have to remember Rachel and her refusal to be consoled, in spite of God's assurance that 'there is hope for your future' (Jer. 31.15). Rachel's lament amidst the broken-hearted people reaches God's ears and her refusal to be placated 'becomes a witness pointing to the Resurrection'.[25] This resurrection hope springs from the well of a caring community. Rachel's lament is a call to communities of faith to incarnate Christ in the midst of broken-heartedness, just as Jesus showed his disciples how to be Christ to each other.

People experience Christ in loving and caring communities that connect hearts with strong bonds of mutuality and reciprocity with power to overcome evil. Brock describes this primal power of interrelatedness as erotic power. Erotic power enables humanity to be open and sensitive to the needs of others, and helps us to be in touch with ourselves. It is the 'sensuous, transformative whole-making wisdom'[26] that arises from the involvement of the heart in relationships. This kind of community is not necessarily Christian, for Jesus declares that he has other sheep outside the fold, and they too, listen to him (John 10.16). Anyone who exemplifies the love of God for peoples and creation embodies Christ.

VII   The challenge and risk of rethinking Incarnation

Rethinking Christology is a challenge. Many people still believe that the timeless truth of doctrines depends on, or is the same thing as, historically-relative wording or concepts. To reformulate them is irreverent and heretical. In his time, Jesus made people see things differently and get out of the tradition-box avidly guarded by the religious leaders. Transgressing suppressive boundaries is a sacred task that opens doors for subjugated knowledge to surface. We have to be courageous enough to acknowledge that the Holy Spirit inspires new possibilities and ways of understanding Incarnation, and steers people away from theological smugness.

The task of rethinking calls people to see theology as dynamic, engaging with the liberating elements of cultures and religions. It needs to be done alongside the practical aspects of ministry: writing curricula, liturgies, hymns, preaching, and other vehicles of teaching. Christology is shaped by the experience and practice of being Christ-incarnate to one another in communities of caring and life-giving wisdom.

Incarnation, being at the centre of Christology, is an unceasing rhythm of the relationship between humanity and God. Believers are called to reveal the just and loving God in their daily lives: in relationships with people and with the Earth. In this light, communities of faith redefine Christology and reclaim the centrality of Incarnation and its moral and religious power in their lives.

Notes

1. It is said that the icon Black Nazarene became black as a result of a fire on the galleon that transported it from Acapulco, Mexico to Manila in the fourteenth century. The Black Nazarene devotees celebrated his feast with a procession in Manila.
2. Legend says the first wooden icon of the child Jesus was a gift of Ferdinand Magellan, the Portuguese mercenary who led the Spanish colonialist expedition, to Juana, the Christianized wife of the Cebu chieftain Rajah Humabon. 'Pit Señor' is a contraction of 'sangpit Señor' or 'Call the Lord'.
3. P. Freire, *Pedagogy of the Oppressed*, New York, 1973.
4. M. Sarup. *An Introductory Guide to Post-Structuralism and Postmodernism*, second ed., n. p., n. d.
5. N. Tuana, *Woman and the History of Philosophy*, St Paul, MN, 1992.
6. Athanasius of Alexandria, 'On the Incarnation of the Word', in Cyril C. Richardson (ed.), *Christology of the Later Fathers*, Louisville, 1954, p. 162.
7. Chung Hyun Kyung, 'Following Naked Dancing and Long Dreaming', in L. Russell, Kwok Pui-lan, A. M. Isasi-Diaz & K. Cannon (eds), *Inheriting Our Mother's Gardens: Feminist Theology in Third World Perspective,* Louisville, KY, 1988, p. 58.
8. Gregory of Nazianzus, 'To Cledonius against Apollinaris' (Epistle 101), in Edward R. Hardy (ed.), *Christology of the Later Fathers*, Louisville, 1954, p. 216.
9. *Ibid.*, p. 218.
10. Brian Hebblethwaite, 'Incarnation', in Joseph L. Price (ed.), *A New Handbook of Christian Theology*, Nashville, 1992, pp. 251–4.
11. R. R. Ruether, *Sexism and God-Talk,* Boston, 1983, pp. 73–4.
12. M. Daly. *Beyond God the Father*, London, 1975, pp. 73–4.
13. J. H. Cone, *God of the Oppressed.* revised ed., Maryknoll, NY, 1997, pp. 101, 125.
14. D. S. Williams, *Sisters in the Wilderness: The Challenge of Womanist God-Talk,* Maryknoll, NY, 1993.
15. V. Fabella, 'Christology from an Asian Woman's Perspective', in R. S. Sugirtharajah (ed.), *Asian Faces of Jesus*, Maryknoll, New York, 1993, p. 212.
16. Kwok Pui-lan, *Introducing Asian Feminist Theology.* Cleveland, OH, 2000, p. 93.
17. Chung Hyun Kyung. *Struggle to Be the Sun Again*, Maryknoll, NY, 1990.
18. M. Althaus-Reid, *Indecent Theology: Theological Perversions in Sex, Gender and Politics*, London & New York, 2000, p. 95.
19. 'The Bhagavad-Gita', IV,1–14, in Dominic Goodall (tr.), *Hindu Scriptures*, Berkeley & Los Angeles, 1996.

20. B. Hebblethwaite, 'Incarnation', *op. cit.*, p. 250.
21. This was in Negros Oriental in the Philippines. The devastating Typhoon Sendong hit the province and two other provinces in Mindanao in December 2012. Then Negros Oriental was rocked by an earthquake swarm in February with a low of 4.1 to a high of 6.9 on the scale. At the time of writing, more than a thousand quakes were recorded by Philippine Volcanology and Seismology.
22. Rene Girard, *Violence and the Sacred*, New York, 2005.
23. C. Morse, *Not Every Spirit: A Dogmatics of Christian Disbelief*, Philadelphia, 1994, p. 11.
24. R. N. Brock. *Journeys by Heart: A Christology of Erotic Power*, New York, 1988, p. 91.
25. C. Morse, *Not Every Spirit, op. cit.*, p. 11.
26. R. N. Brock, *Journeys by Heart, op. cit*, p. 26.

The Trinity
Gender and the Role of Dissonance

PATRICIA A. FOX

I Introduction

In a recent publication, John McGuckin, a patristic theologian, traces a path through the complexities of the earliest articulations of the doctrine of the Trinity by encouraging the reader to imagine the journey as five great acts of a play. He describes the dramas of the first four acts as they unfolded until the fifth century and as they were completed later by the creative work of the eighth-century theologian John Damascene. McGuckin describes these acts as 'startling because of the speed and variety with which schools of thought of this time spun out new reflections on the deeply mysterious ideas about God and his action in the cosmos'. These acts, grounded in the Scriptures and the liturgical mysteries of the Christian community are 'fluid and inter-reactive'. He describes Act Five as 'the bemused aftermath, a long quieting-down as the Trinity becomes a fixed dogma, a quieting that often lapses into silence'.[1] This vivid and slightly tongue-in-cheek sketch can help situate the revival of the doctrine of the Trinity of recent decades against the wider horizon of the development of the doctrine. It can also serve to situate the recent emergence of feminist theology. It brings to mind two key factors that are largely missing within the development of Trinitarian theology over all these centuries. Both are related to gender. One is the absence of women's active contribution to the development of this central doctrine of God. The other is a failure to value the role of dissonance in talk about God.

Over the last few decades, there has been a small but significant shift in the imbalance of women's contribution to the reclaiming of the mystery of the Trinity and further developments have followed from feminist theologians' work on biblical, historical, patristic, liturgical and spiritual sources, and from contemporary disciplines such as sociology and psychology.²

In this article on gender and Trinity, I shall focus on three elements in a renewed Trinitarian theology, which are essential for authentic reception of the full riches of the triune mystery. One has to do with attending to women's voices and experiences; another with the need to ensure that many names, images (including female imaging) and metaphors for God are accessed; and a third with the need to value cognitive dissonance as an essential tool in Trinitarian discourse.

In conjunction with the foregoing, I shall examine the Trinitarian theology of Julian of Norwich as a primary source. Whereas Julian's spiritual writings have been valued by many, like the writings of most mystics, they have not been generally received as a *locus theologicus*, or as a serious contribution to Trinitarian theology.⁴ It seems fitting that an article on *Trinity and Gender* should at least point the reader in the direction of this creative English theologian, who so many centuries ago harnessed the dissonant power of language to uncover some of the deeper mysteries of the triune God with great power and tenderness. Julian has begun to receive recognition as a Trinitarian theologian only in more recent times. I shall begin with some relevant observations by a contemporary English theologian.

II Cognitive and affective dissonance as an entry into holy mystery

Sarah Coakley goes to the heart of the patristic sources described by McGuckin in order to examine the contradictions and ambiguities of language that are necessary to appreciate the mystery of God and of self. She focuses, for example, on the work of Gregory of Nyssa and shows that the process of human transformation is the Trinity's very point of intersection with our lives. She suggests that any such transformation requires 'profound, even alarming shifts in our gender perceptions, shifts which have bearing as much on our thinking about God as about our understanding of ourselves'.⁵ Coakley refers to Gregory of Nyssa's late work, the *Commentary on the Song of* Songs, where he 'charts in the highly imagistic and eroticized language, the ascent of the soul into the intimacy of the Trinity'. She observes that Gregory wants us to understand that if we are to advance to a deep intimacy with the Trinitarian God, 'gender stereotypes must be reversed, undermined, and transcended; and ...the language of sexuality and gender, far from being an optional aside or mere rhetorical flourish in the process, is somehow necessary and intrinsic to the epistemological deepening that Gregory seeks to describe'.[6] She shows how Gregory realizes, with a mystic's clarity, that Trinitarian doctrine does not strictly speaking *describe* God.[7] For Coakley, the discomfort and destabilization effected by the use of such imagery and language invite us into a liminal sacred space and enable us to enter into Holy Mystery.

She addresses the issue of gender from a different perspective when she focuses on the Pauline vision in Galatians 3.28, 'neither male *and* female'. In this case, she argues that maleness and femaleness are rendered spiritually insignificant in the face of the Spirit's work and our transformations into Christ's body.[8] Both of these perspectives illustrate a basic point she makes about the way gender has been used theologically and spiritually in a static manner in order to maintain the *status quo*. Like the creative theologians responsible for our inherited expression of the Trinitarian dogma, Coakley works from the premiss that if you try to talk about the One who is infinite and incomprehensible, you must value, rather than fear the cognitive dissonance and destabilization of set paradigms created by the interplay of contradictory images from multiple sources. She is convinced that prayer and entering the place of contemplation can free a person to stay with the profound ambiguities and disquiet involved in approaching the living God. The writings and witness of Julian, an anchoress in medieval Norwich, can provide this kind of invitation for pilgrims and theologians seeking to enter the life of the Trinity today.

III The showings of Julian of Norwich (1373–1423)

Denys Turner describes Julian's text as 'one of the most exhilarating, moving, disturbing works of theology in any age'.[9] In 1373, when Julian was in her thirty-first year and appeared to be at the point of death, she received a profound religious experience of entering into Jesus' death and resurrection. Having prayed for the grace of the 'mind of the passion', she experienced a jarring dissonance as she witnessed an innocent man tortured and killed in series of 'bodily sightes' or visions, while at the same time experiencing herself as a woman dying.[10] She records this transformative experience in the first person in vernacular Middle English. Her account is intended for the baptized rather than specifically for the ordained or for those in monastic life. She speaks with authority and communicates a strong sense of being guided in her work. She tells us that: 'For twenty years after the time of the revelation except three months, I received an inward instruction.'[11] For years Julian lived, questioned and prayed into this distressing and confronting event. With rigour and courage she questioned its meaning in the light of the Scriptures and the classic theological sources of the tradition of the time available to her. Turner, who describes Julian as a systematic theologian, goes to the heart of her work, when he observes that: 'It is perhaps Julian's central theological insight that sin wages war against love, because sin is of its own nature violent, but love wages no wars at all, not even against sin, for love is absolute vulnerability. Love knows no other strategy than vulnerability...In its victory over love sin defeats itself. Sin's failure to engage perfect love in a contest on sin's terms of violence and power is sin's defeat, its power being exhausted by its very success. For killing is the best strategy that sin can come up with; it is sin's last resort. The Resurrection then is the meaning of the Cross, the meaning of the vulnerability of love.'[12]

Julian's thought never wavers because of the certainty at the centre of her work that 'Love is the meaning'.[13] This utter conviction resolves the seemingly impossible paradox that an omnipotent love could create a world in which evil and sin can exist. She witnesses the raw pain of Jesus being killed by evil and understands that in so doing he gives birth to the victory of a vulnerable love over death for all humankind for eternity. In this sense, she experiences and knows Jesus as our mother of mercy, who feeds us with his body and blood.

Kerrie Hide's article on 'the Deep Wisdom of Christ Our Mother'[14] from the writings of Julian of Norwich acknowledges that, while the image of divine motherhood is not unique, Julian's application of this image to the Trinity is arguably unparalleled in the Christian tradition. Moreover, Julian applies the title 'Jesus our Mother' with sophistication, depth and coherence. Hide begins her article on Julian's Trinitarian theology by sketching the extensive provenance of the image of the salvific role of Christ as mother in both Eastern and Western traditions, and then focuses on the precedents for the two metaphors of *wisdom* and *mother* in Augustine. She concludes that there is evidence that Julian had received grounding 'in some type of Augustinian synthesis that enables her to develop her theology in continuity with the established tradition'.[15]

Julian's work places the source of humanity within God and establishes that our being is totally derived from Christ. She describes God conceiving of human existence in relation to Christ who, as our loving mother, acts within human experience and bears and nurtures a capacity within humankind for a joy that is eternal. Hide notes that, in contrast to Augustine, Julian harnesses the dynamic of the interrelated imagery of wisdom and mother to create a dialectical tension uniting both aspects of Christ's meaning for us. She talks of 'the deep wisdom of the Trinity our Mother' In order to depict human beings enclosed within God's triune self: 'For the almyghty truth of the trynyte is oure fader, for he made vs and kepyth vs in hym. And the depe wysdome of the trynyte is our mader, in whom we be closyd. And the hye goodnesse of the trynyte is our lord, and in hym we be closyd and he in vs.'[16]

Hide emphasizes that by locating motherhood in the deep wisdom of the Trinity, 'Julian demonstrates that motherhood is not only attributed to the salvific work of Christ in historical time but that it is eternally grounded within the deep centre of God'.[17] Her anthropology shows that there is an intimate connection between human beings and the God in whom we are enclosed by divine love. Motherhood is thus depicted as emanating from the very nature of God. Drawing on the Book of Wisdom and 1 Corinthians, where Christ is called both the power of God and the wisdom of God, Julian portrays Christ as mother wisdom forever active in creation. Wisdom incarnate personifies and gives life to attributes of wisdom in human nature. In this way, Julian vividly portrays God in Christ substantially present in the very flesh and spirit of humanity: 'And ferthere more I saw that the seconde person, whych is oure moder, subtanncyally the same derewurthy person, is now become oure moder sensuall, for we be doubell of gods makyng, that is to sey substanniciall and sensuall.'[18]

For Julian, grace is experiential, concrete and historical. She creates a list of the qualities of Mother Christ, describing how he feeds us with himself: 'The moder may geue her chylde sucke hyr mylke, but oure precyous moder Jhesu, he may fede vs wyth hym selfe, and dothe full curtesly and full tenderyrly with the blessyd sacrament, that is precyous fode of very lyfe'.[19] Hide comments that 'as we participate in Trinitarian life through the deep wisdom of the Trinity our mother, we encounter spiritual birth in our sensuality through the careful responsive nurturing of Christ'.[20] Julian thus makes the images of wisdom and mother interdependent to reveal that human beings eternally born in God can trust in a love that is eternally present.

Reflecting on the theological implications of Julian's soteriology, Hide observes that when Julian attributes motherhood to Christ's work in history, she finds its source within the very nature of God. This can give humanity a new understanding of how creatures are born of God: 'Christ images a two-fold feminine manifestation of the divinity, wisdom and mother, and the male physical form of Jesus of Nazareth. Thereby all human beings, male or female can see themselves reflected in Christ. In Julian's soteriology, the mother–wisdom image works with the maleness of Christ to emphasize that Christ gives birth to the complete humanity, male and female. Therefore all humankind, regardless of gender, has the potential for participating in the divine nature by being oned to Christ.'[21]

Further, because Mother Wisdom is the paradigm of all wisdom and knowledge, yet also nurtures us as a mother would physically attend to a child, the values of the intellect and of a generous compassion extend to both men and women. Christ understood as the divine exemplar enables Julian to subvert classic gender distinctions that equate the masculine principle with the intellect and the feminine principle with affectivity. The wisdom-mother link also suggests that the love of God in creating the world extends to eternity. Hence Julian's utter conviction proclaimed with such authority that 'all will be well'.[22]

Julian does not seek to substitute motherhood for fatherhood. For her, they are not opposed or mutually exclusive. Rather, both together contribute to a deeper appreciation of the fullness of the mystery of God's Trinitarian self. The dissonance thus created assists the reception of this doctrine. Jean Leclercq suggests that what makes Julian's use of the image God as Mother unique is 'the theological precision with which she applies this symbolism to Trinitarian relationships.' He further claims that '[t]here is here a full theology of Trinitarian life.'[23] In theological discourse, the embrace of one aspect of Christian dogma can often lead to the neglect or even the denial or of other aspects. This is sometimes particularly prevalent within Trinitarian discourse. Yet the heart of a theology of one God as a communion of three divine Persons is precisely about difference in communion.

The very experience of unease occasioned by dissonance in discourse on the Trinity can remind theologians and believers of the analogous character of all statements about God. The Showings of Julian of Norwich offer contemporary readers the possibility of a schooling in this liberating role of dissonance, which not only challenges all gender stereotypes but leads us into deeper insights into the mystery of the incomprehensible God.

The Trinity: Gender and the Role of Dissonance

Notes

1. J. A. McGuckin, 'The Trinity in the Greek Fathers', in P. C. Phan (ed.), *The Cambridge Companion to The Trinity*, Cambridge, 2011, p. 49.
2. I. Gebara, *Longing for Running Water: Ecofeminism and Liberation*, Minneapolis, 1999; S. Coakley, 'The Trinity, Prayer and Sexuality', in J. M. Soskice & D. Lipton (Eds), *Feminism & Theology: Oxford Readings in Theology*. Oxford, 2003; *id.*, 'The Trinity and Gender Reconsidered', in M. Volf & M. Welker (eds). *God's Life in the Trinity*, Minneapolis, 2006; *id.*, '"Persons" in the "Social" doctrine of the Trinity: a Critique of Current Analytic Discussion', in S. T. Davis, D. Kendall SJ & G. O'Collins SJ (eds), *The Trinity: An Interdisciplinary Symposium on the Trinity*, Oxford, 1999; C. M. Lacugna, *God for Us: The Trinity and Christian Life*. New York, 1991; E. Johnson, *She Who Is: The Mystery of God in Feminist Theological Discourse*, New York, 1992.
3. See P. A. Fox, 'Feminist Theologies and the Trinity', in P. C. Phan (ed.), *Cambridge Companion, op. cit.*, pp. 274–90.
4. A. Hunt, *The Trinity; Insights From the Mystics*, Collegeville, 2010, pp. 115–6.
5. S. Coakley, 'Persons', *op. cit.*, p. 125.
6. *Ibid.*, p. 142.
7. S. Coakley, 'Why Three?', *op. cit.*, p. 47.
8. S. Coakley, 'The Trinity and Gender', *op. cit.*, p. 140.
9. D. Turner, *Julian of Norwich: Theologian*, Yale, 2011, p. xix.
10. *Ibid.*, p. xiii.
11. E. Colledge & J. Walsh (eds), *Julian of Norwich: Showings*, New York, 1978, p. 270.
12. D. Turner, *Julian, op. cit.*, p. 21.
13. E. Colledge & J. Walsh, *Showings, op. cit.*, p. 342.
14. Kerrie Hide, 'The Deep Wisdom of Christ Our Mother: Echoes in Augustine and Julian of Norwich', *The Australasian Catholic Record* 4 (1997), pp. 434–44.
15. See K. Hide, *op. cit.*, pp. 432–4.
16. *Ibid.*, pp. 437–8. Quotations are from E. Colledge & J. Walsh, *A Book of Showings to the Anchoress Julian of Norwich*, Toronto, 1978. All quotations are from the long text – revelation number, chapter and page number: LT 14: 54, pp. 20–4. Translations are from E. Colledge & J. Walsh, *Showings, op. cit.*, p. 285. 'For the almighty truth of the Trinity is our Father, for he made us and keeps us in him. And the deep wisdom of the Trinity is our Mother, in whom we are enclosed. And the high goodness of the Trinity is our Lord, and in him we are enclosed and he in us'.
17. K. Hide, *op. cit.*, p. 438.
18. *Ibid.*, p. 440. LT 14: 58, pp. 36–40. 'And furthermore I saw that the second person who is our Mother, substantially the same beloved person, has now become our Mother sensually, because we are double by God's creating, that is to say substantial and sensual', p. 294.
19. *Ibid.*, pp. 441–2. LT14: 60 29–32. 'The mother can give her child to suck of her milk, but our precious mother Jesus can feed us with himself, and does most courteously and most tenderly, with the blessed sacrament, which is the precious food of true life', 298.
20. *Ibid.*, p. 442.
21. *Ibid.*, p. 443.
22. E. Colledge & J. Walsh, *Showings, op. cit.*, p. 151.
23. *Ibid.*, pp. 9–10.

Liberating Renunciation
Reflections on Contemporary
Feminist Spirituality

SUSAN M. ST VILLE

Always attentive to history, gender theory has consistently shown that tracing the (often contested) development of concepts over time leads to a deeper understanding of the questions opening before us in the present moment. To address the topic of gender and spirituality, and more narrowly the possibilities for a contemporary Christian feminist spirituality, it is helpful to glance back over past articulations and hopes for this field of study and practice. The boom of feminist theology in the 1970s and 1980s brought with it inspiring visions of a decidedly liberatory feminist spirituality. This vision took different forms, of course, but Anne Carr's view captures much of what was common: '…a feminist spirituality is that mode of relating to God (and everyone and everything in relationship to God) exhibited by those who are deeply aware of the historical and cultural restriction of women to a narrowly defined "place" within the wider human (male) world.'[1] If spirituality is the personal relationship of the self to the divine, then a feminist spirituality indicates the relationship of a specifically *feminist* self to the divine. Rooted in a feminist consciousness, this spiritual interaction would yield personal transformation for the believer and bear implications for her political actions in the world. Carr characterizes the personal transformation as one of self-empowerment, noting that, through worship, the believer 'would strive for an ever freer, but always human, self-transcendence before a God who does not call us servants but friends'.[2] The egalitarian ethos of the relationship to the divine carries over as a model for relationships in the world inspiring the believer to stand against those structures of oppression that seek to delimit individual freedom.

Liberating Renuniciation

What is striking from the current vantage point, some 30 years later, are the assumptions, particularly about the value of a free and transcendent self, which underlie this optimistic vision of feminist spirituality. For, in the years that followed these formulations, gender theorists, particularly those with a post-structuralist perspective, roundly criticized the legitimacy of the liberal self. This critique, arguably most pointedly put forth in the writings of Judith Butler, brought significant epistemological challenges to the feminist theological project, resulting in an important reassessment of its goals and possibilities.[3] In what follows, I shall explore some of the questions these analytical attacks raise for Christian feminist spirituality. Drawing on the writings of Judith Butler to represent this challenge, I shall ask more fully what it means to think of a self in relation to the divine when the notion of the self is radically in question. How are we left to conceptualize the agency or personal transformation fostered within a feminist spirituality? Further, what are the implications of the loss of identity for the political efficacy of this spirituality?

It is important to stress that this is more than a theoretical exercise, for challenges to a feminist spirituality narrowly construed come not only from the analytical realm. The lived spiritual practices of many women run counter to the vision of spirituality that valorizes the free and liberal self. Traditional forms of worship in all religious traditions are often based on principles of self-renunciation. While we might recognize the risks of these practices, they nonetheless continue to be deeply familiar and deeply meaningful to many women who engage in them, an observation that might lead us to ask if we have fully grasped how these practices are shaping those who find inspiration in them. Saba Mahmood, in her anthropological study of women in the Egyptian Mosque Movement, has written movingly of this reality in the Islamic context.[4] There women adopt actions such as wearing a veil, moving the body in a deferential manner and modulating the voice that are intentionally meant to foster dispositions of docility or shyness. These dispositions, which seemingly run counter to feminist ideals of empowerment, represent the height of aspirations to piety in this context. Mahmood argues that to assess these practices with pre-determined political categories privileging the free and independent self leads us to dismiss them too easily as curtailing women's agency, and to miss the nuances of the capacity for action and formation of the self they engender in faithful believers.

Within Christianity too, we find many women for whom practices of renunciation and dispositions of subordination are part and parcel of their spiritual practice. As a clinician working with women who have suffered abusive violence or rape, I have often heard clients speak of their faith commitments in ways that may sound like the extreme form of this spiritual stance. Different feminist theologians have noted the confluence between women who have suffered extreme violence and the figure of Christ on the cross.[5] In these accountings, the emphasis is generally on the comfort that comes to victims who feel they are not alone in their suffering and that the crucified Christ engenders in them the ability to survive the ordeal. And yet, often what I hear from the women with whom I talk includes another haunting moment, one in which women experience a powerful feeling of the absence of God in their suffering. In what I have come to think of as a 'spirituality of radical acceptance',[6] women speak of the feeling of being abandoned, coupled with a deep sense that they are called to accept this abandonment. Here, it is the forsaken Christ of Gethsemane who is the model and the prayer, 'let it be done according to your will' sounds as the epitome of the passive renunciation of the self.

The challenge for me is how to listen and respond to these statements, a challenge which rests on determining what these women are expressing in terms of the spiritual agency they find through this practice of radically deferring their own will to the divine. Clearly, different feminist theoretical frameworks suggest different interpretations. If I listen with 'liberal feminist' ears, that is, with criteria shaped by the ideal of the autonomous and self-determining subject, these spiritual statements bear the tell-tale marks of a 'false consciousness'. From this angle, these can only be heard as the words of a woman who has internalized oppression and whose practices of subordination to the divine reinforce and are complicit with her own abuse. My response then would probably be to encourage the woman to move beyond this spiritual stance to develop a more solid sense of self in relationship to God and the world. A first difficulty with this response is that in questioning the woman's construal of her spiritual state, I risk re-enacting the dynamic of oppression in our relationship by suggesting that she take on my ideal of her subjectivity rather than her own. And further, in my experience, this interpretation misses the complexity of what I seem to hear from my clients. Understanding this as a simply passive spirituality belies the note of resilience and the incipient strength that sounds in the woman's claim to hold together radical faith and radical absence.

It is here that the analytical framework provided by Butler in her theory of performative subjectivity offers a different way to approach these claims that is perhaps better able to capture their nuances. Rather than measuring the woman's words against a pre-determined conception of a liberated subject, Butler calls us to begin with the speech itself, tracing the path of its development and the particular capacities for action that emerge from the practices it enacts and advocates. While it is not possible to give an exhaustive accounting of Butler's theory, I will in what follows review two of its key aspects, namely the concept of reiteration and the emphasis on language as utterance, in order to suggest how it might open the way for a new hearing of the spirituality of radical acceptance.

As a thinker firmly in the constructivist tradition, Butler consistently denies the existence of a liberal or transcendent self that stands apart from the shaping power of cultural norms and social expectations. Adamant that the subject results from the working of social discourse, Butler seeks in the theory of performativity to describe more precisely the way in which this formation or materialization of the subject takes place. To do so, she turns to contemporary language theory to conceptualize the workings of social discourse. Butler notes that in our common-sense perception (one that is wedded to the notion of the liberal subject) we understand the subject's relationship to the social order along the lines mapped out by descriptive language. Here a subject uses language to make a statement about an external reality. This linguistic form assumes a subject who pre-exists and has full power of choice over the use of, and engagement with, discourse. In contrast, Butler's theory asserts that the formation of the gendered subject is captured more adequately by a different linguistic form, that of the performative utterance.[7] Following Austin and Derrida, Butler understands performative language not as statements that point to a pre-existing reality but rather as statements that produce the reality about which they speak. In short, these are illocutionary acts that 'do what they say' and in so doing produce a new state of affairs. Performative statements have traditionally been recognized most obviously in official pronouncements. Thus, the proclamation: 'You are under arrest' yelled by the policeman who apprehends a thief enacts a new reality – in this case to move a subject from a free to a bound state.

In describing the process of subject formation, Butler argues that even the most ostensibly descriptive statements are better understood as performative. When a person states, 'I am a woman', we tend to view this claim as describing a stable reality and in so doing miss the ways in which the saying of the words in actuality gives rise to or produces the subject, who is then recognizable as a woman. Butler characterizes the process of performativity as one of reiteration in which time and again accepted social norms are cited and recited, enacted and re-enacted. In saying, 'I am a woman', or in continually practising the behaviours, dress or demeanours deemed appropriate for a woman, the subject emerges according to the prescribed and accepted identity, as what culture considers to be a woman. Rather than a pre-existent reality, the subject is instead an effect of the active working of social norms, which recognize certain types of subjectivity even as they foreclose on or fail to recognize other possibilities. Far from being an autonomous subject with a free will, subjectivity is always in some manner a function of subjectivation to norms prescribing what will be acknowledged as a subject.[8]

This characterization of subject formation as subjectivation seems to leave little room for liberatory action, let alone transcendent self-consciousness. Butler suggests otherwise, and the significance of the emphasis on reiteration comes into play in her description of transformative or resistant subjectivity. As historical and contingent, cultural norms have a certain power to determine subjectivity but this power is not absolute. The norms themselves depend on the repeated use or repetition in order to wield their power. The phrase 'You are under arrest' is effective only because in each evocation it is recognized by those involved as carrying the power to bind the thief. With every reiteration, the possibility is opened that the norm might be enacted differently. The thief might fail to yield to the policeman's call, and with regard to gendered expectations a person might walk with a slightly different gait or gesture in a slightly different style and, if successful, in the process generate a new form of subjectivity.

Drag performances provide Butler's classic example of unexpected reiteration. Here we see the socially-sanctioned dress and movement of a woman enacted, our expectations are met and a subject with the gender identity of a woman materializes before us. And yet, the exposure of the drag shows that in this iteration the identity is linked with an unexpected physical anatomy. What had been prescribed by the norms (namely the norm linking gender and sex) is undermined. The unexpected inhabiting of the norm reveals that the state of affairs we had accepted as natural is subject to change. And, with the failing of the illusion of the natural, the horizon is open for us to entertain and accept alternative normative configurations and alternative subjects.

This emphasis that roots transformative subjectivity in acts of reiteration points the way towards a different interpretation of the spiritual practices of submission. In offering her own will to God, the woman is taking on a norm common to Christian believers. Experience leads us to assume that this renders her powerless, placing her squarely in the position of the victim. But, in stating and re-stating 'let it be done according to your will', perhaps the woman is enacting the norm in a manner counter to our expectations, one that opens for her an agency that is also unexpected.

To see how repeated submission to God might foster a distinct form of subjectivity, it is useful to pause to consider that Butler's move from the descriptive to the performative is also a move to the active utterance, that is from viewing language as a statement made (the said) to concentrating on the dynamic movement of language between subjects (the saying). If the subject is created in and through the use of the norms, this occurs only because this enactment of norms entails the forging of a relationship. Austin noted that the meaning of a performative utterance depends not on its accuracy when measured against an external reality but on its 'felicity' – how it sounds and is received by those who hear the utterance.[9] If each utterance is a bid to the other, a reaching out of sorts, the meaning depends on how fully the gesture is grasped and responded to, how deeply the connection is made.

Viewed in this light, through the utterance of renunciation – 'let it be done to me according to your will' – the woman may be viewed as both enacting renunciation and reaching out to the divine in an effort (however negative) to compel a response. To better understand the quality of the relationship between a radically-humbled self and the divine, and the fragile agency that it produces, it is useful to recall the familiar traditions of negative theology. In the *Divine Names*, Dionysus reminds us that even those words that seem to most fully capture the revelations of the divine must be held gently.[10] Whatever affirmations we might make in naming the divine are most properly accompanied by their negation. Through the indeterminate play of assertion and denial language opens to the God, who in superabundance, lies beyond all affirmation and negation. If the *Divine Names* meditates on our descriptive words for God, it also sets the stage for understanding prayerful utterance directed to God. Bernard McGinn suggests that the unknowing of Dionysius 'is not a "'what" at all, not some concept or content that can be described or defined. It is more like a state of mind (if only in a paradoxical way) – the subjective correlative to the objective unknowability of God'.[11] Negativity inflects the relationship forged in the prayerful utterance with a particular quality. In full acknowledgement of its inadequacy, human identity falters before the divine, for to insist on self-possession would serve to limit what might be exchanged in the interaction. When the woman reaches out through the renunciation of control, she positions herself as open and readied for the fullest possible response from the divine.

Given this construal of the subjectivity forged through the practice of submission, what are the implications for the feminist dream of a liberatory spirituality, one in which the relationship to the divine in turn empowers the believer's ability to counter worldly injustice? It can seem as if the survivor of violence who has surrendered her own will is at best rendered unable to act on her own behalf and at worst is made a target for further abuse. It is true that negative spirituality is not without hazards for those who have suffered oppression.[12] And, I am not advocating a simple passivity much less acquiescence to continued violation at the hands of others. The manner in which we stand up against violence, however, need not be limited to steeling ourselves for the zero-sum game of direct confrontation. The resilience that sounds in my client's voices, I believe, is rather the faith that the divine will offer the transforming love necessary for every new situation, securing the self for a time but also undoing the self toward further growth when appropriate. This spirituality is liberatory, not only because it inspires work for justice but also because it liberates us from taking the battle of resistance as the exclusive focus of feminist identity. Beyond these obvious struggles, we may remain faithfully open to the unpredictable and unpredictably transforming political engagements that allow for the continuing growth in love.

Notes

1. Carr, 'On Feminist Spirituality' in J. Wolski Conn (ed.), *Women's Spirituality: Resources for Christian Development*, New York, 1986, pp. 53–4.
2. *Ibid.*, p. 55.
3. See E. Armour and S. St Ville (eds), *Bodily Citations*, New York, 2006.
4. Saba Mahmood, *Politics of Piety: The Islamic Revival and the Feminist Subject*, Princeton, 2005.
5. See for example E. Johnson, *She Who Is: The Mystery of God in Feminist Theological Discourse*, New York, 2002, pp. 269–72.

6. For a further psychological discussion on radical acceptance, see M. Linehan, *Cognitive-Behavioral Treatment of Borderline Personality Disorder*, New York, p. 148.
7. Butler's theory of performativity is most classically presented in J. Butler, *Gender Trouble: Feminism and the Subversion of Identity*, New York, 1990. For more on her use of J. L. Austin, see J. Butler, *Bodies that Matter: On the Discursive Limits of Sex*, New York, 1993, p. 2.
8. For subject formation as subjectivation, see especially J. Butler, *The Psychic Life of Power: Theories in Subjection*, Stanford, 1997.
9. J. L. Austin, *How to Do Things with Words*, J. O. Urmson & M. Sbisa (eds), Cambridge, 1962, pp. 18–9.
10. Pseudo-Dionysius, 'The Divine Names', in *Pseudo-Dionysius: The Complete Works*, trans. Colm Luibheid & Paul Rorem, New York, 1987.
11. B. McGinn, *The Foundations of Mysticism: Origins to the Fifth Century*, New York, 1991, p. 175.
12. For a further discussion of negative theology and its risks, see M. Jordan, *Telling Truths in Church: Scandal, Flesh, and Christian Spirituality*, Boston, 2003.

Gender and Ecclesiology
Authorities, Structures, Ministry

ANNE ARABOME SSS

I Introduction

How is it that Christianity has offered freedom and liberation to women and, at the same time, the chains of oppression? On the one hand, the teachings of the Church have elevated the position and status of women, recognizing women as deserving respect and reverence. On the other hand, 'women presently experience a Christianity that has, with its Church and through its theology, decisively contributed toward the development of a destructively intolerant patriarchal society'.[1] The negative consequences of patriarchal attitudes and structures manifest themselves in church ministries all over the world, to say nothing of women's negative conceptualizations regarding their own bodies.

II Ecclesiology

When it comes to the theological understanding of the Church, the views of scholasticism, under the aegis of Aquinas, have had a predominant influence. Vatican II opened the musty windows of crusted thinking and brought fresh perspectives into the understanding of the nature and mission of the Church. In theory, at least, it dismantled the model of pyramidal hierarchy. The pilgrim people of God became a compelling description of the Church. Richard McBrien considers feminist, liberationist, and ethnic ecclesiologies as positive developments within the post-Vatican II Church, along with the emergence of lay associations and movements.[2] Since Vatican II, the people of God have been searching for new ways to experience their commitment to God in contemporary terms.

McBrien also notes the emergence of small base communities as a new expression of Church, drawing from the lives of the poor in understanding the message of Christ as Liberator. These small communities 'are Eucharistic communities within the Church...Their members pray together, minister to one another ... and collaborate in works of justice and charity'.[3] This confirms the long-held conviction of liberation theologians, like Leonardo Boff, that small base communities act as a call to the institution because they acknowledge the presence of each individual and eliminate structures of dominance by interacting in free flowing relationships. They live the message of Jesus by helping each other and challenging the inequities around them. Each person is recognized for his or her giftedness regardless of gender.[4] The implications for women's role and involvement in the Church are transformational!

However, considering the current state of the Church's hierarchical governance and its structures, women ask: Where do women fit as members of the body of Christ? Given the reality of unequal treatment, how do we correct the gender imbalance? Scholars, especially feminist theologians, have written extensively about issues of gender in regards to Church and society and the painful exclusion of women from church leadership, authority, and ministries.

The image of God as male serves as the starting-point of this exclusion. We have only to turn to the Hebrew Scriptures to glimpse the highly patriarchal Jewish culture from which these books were written. The Pauline letters and the writings of the church Fathers (Tertullian, Augustine) emphasized the inferiority of women and reinforced negative stereotypes of femininity. There is some counterbalance in Pauline writings that speak of the house churches and the leadership of women in these churches, as partners in ministry. However, in the end, religion, society, and culture continue to confine women – almost universally – to a status of subjugation and oppression. Colonization and slavery have exacerbated this oppression, while the modern media relentlessly propagate age-old stereotypes of women. In this regard, the Christian Church has mimicked culture. Thus, even within a religion that acknowledges Christ as Liberator, women continue to be treated as second-class human beings. Understandably, women must take the lead to explore and probe 'how social constructions of sex/gender, race, colonialism, class and religion have influenced and shaped theoretical frameworks, theoretical formulations, and biblical interpretations'.[5]

III Universal pain of women: a tale of two worlds

An African proverb says: 'A human being is a human being through other persons'. It is safe to say that the pain of exclusion for women in our Church is universal, albeit in differing degrees. This is why solidarity between women the world over in view of their liberation is of utmost importance.

In the global North, women are asking for *equality* and full participation in the life and mission of the Church, while women in the global South are struggling to reclaim their *humanity* in the Church and society that have dehumanized them and denied their God-given potential. I recall reading Elizabeth Johnson's *The Church Women Want* during doctoral studies. It triggered a deep pain, knowing that the issues raised in the book by Western middle-class women were not those of African women. The women in the global South experience exclusion and multiple layers of oppression as a consequence of colonialism, poverty, and culture. Uniquely, therefore, 'African feminism combines racial, sexual, class, and cultural dimensions of oppression to produce a more inclusive brand of feminism through which women are viewed first and foremost as *human*, rather than sexual beings'.[6] Though the women of the global South have yet to accomplish this, our sisters in the global North must not presume to speak for our sisters in the global South as though it were possible to do a better job than we could do for ourselves.[7] Women in Africa, Latin America, and Asia must find their own voice and speak their own truths.

While women in the global North may complain about the lack of leadership positions in the Church, those in the global South find no place at all to use their gifts due to gender inequality in the Church. Moreover, women in the global South are burdened by the ravages of war, migration, poverty, violence, rape, and life-threatening cultural practices.

In the global North, women protest when their lives are collapsed to the standards of white male supremacy and their dignity and self-worth are demeaned by negative portrayals in the media. Jane Fonda's lament echoes strongly: 'Media creates consciousness, and if what gets out there that creates our consciousness is determined by men, we (women) are not going to make any progress'.[8] Though our lament echoes from different ends of the globe, our pain as women runs deep. We must reach out and join hands in mutual support.

IV Authority

In the Post-Synodal Apostolic Exhortation, *Africae munus*, Benedict XVI affirms that 'Scripture testifies that the blood which Christ shed for us becomes, through Baptism, the principle and bond of a new fraternity...the very antithesis of division, tribalism, racism and ethnocentrism (cf. Gal. 3.26–8)'.[9] As a woman reflecting on this Galatians text, I would expand the list to include sexism, clericalism, patriarchy, gender inequality, and gender-based violence. How Church is defined is closely related to the understanding of gender. Roman Catholic theological construction is gender biased. Elizabeth Johnson points out that addressing God 'in the exclusive and literal terms of the patriarch is a tool of subtle conditioning that operates to debilitate women's sense of dignity, power, and self-esteem'.[10] Similarly, Elisabeth Schüssler Fiorenza observes that 'the theological problem at hand then is whether the construct of "apostolic succession" of the twelve can be maintained today in view of the historical recognition that the twelve apostles had no successors, nor any priestly ordination'.[11] Jon Sobrino adds that Jesus was a lay person who had no need for 'sacral' power. Rather, Jesus had the qualities of a good and virtuous human being – 'mercy, faithfulness and submission'.[12]

Obviously, patriarchal ecclesial domination varies from place to place. However, in Africa, bishops and clergy are lionized as kings, princes, and potentates. Women serve them and, in doing so, women must hide the reality of their personal power and their gifts of leadership. In this context, 'a priest or bishop can turn into a lifelong oppressor of the ecclesial community, effectively dechristianizing it'.[13] This hierarchical obsession with power violates the Gospel understanding of authority as humble, self-sacrificing service (see Matt. 20.26–8).[14] The question then arises: What was Jesus' relationship to authority? It seems that the kind of authority that Jesus embraced was the authority of love and invitation. His relationship with God showed profound intimacy and faith that enabled him to resist and overcome the forces of evil.[15] On the evidence of the Scriptures, Jesus was introducing an upside-down kind of authority validated by serving others. Schillebeeckx's insight is relevant: 'If you hold office, you have the prophetic function of proclaiming the Gospel of Jesus, in other words, of proclaiming justice. So, wherever there is injustice, you have to oppose it and that means you have to oppose it first of all in the Church itself...

All those who live the life of the Gospel are bound to judge the hierarchy of the Church as a power'.[16]

V Structures

Lisa Cahill asserts that 'the new visibility of women's experience seems, if anything, to have widened the ruptures in the unity of the Church, proving that unity for which many nostalgically yearn is an illusion'.[17] How could such unity be achieved when the structure of the ecclesia is patriarchal and hierarchical, excluding women on account of gender? Yet one could consider this 'new visibility' of women as impetus to challenge patriarchal structures and eliminate discriminatory practices that oppress women in the Church.

Theological statements and official pronouncements about the role of women in Church and society have consistently and unjustly denied women's ability to lead and minister fully. Such eminent personages as Augustine, Tertullian, and Aquinas have muted the authority of women to define themselves. The results have been catastrophic. As Diana Hayes has observed, this situation has 'left women with no right to control their own bodies, minds, offspring, and even their very souls. However, these interpretations took an even more sinister turn when applied to black bodies and minds, whether male or female'.[18] These attitudes towards women in general and, in particular, women of colour, present the Church of Christ with a very serious moral challenge. There is an urgency in this regard, especially as it relates to African women. As Benedict XIV has said, 'the Church and society need women to take their full place in the World "so that the human race can live in the world without completely losing its humanity"'.[19] Yet the structures of the Church, which resemble the economic structures of our world, place women in the global South at the very bottom of the hierarchical pyramid, oblivious of 'the fact that eighty per cent of church membership in Africa is made up of women, and…not even five per cent of church leadership is women'.[20]

The structures of the Church thrive on power and control. Jesus, in contrast, accepted each person not on the basis of wealth and prestige, but on the simple faith that each person embodies the image of God – *'Imago Dei'*. The ecclesial community will only begin to be true to its essence if its structures are based on the respect and the dignity of the human person rather than on control and a fight for positions of authority. As Oduyoye notes, 'The Church must become a household in which all count, and in which the full range of ministries become the joint responsibility of all in the Church'.[21]

VI Ministries

Jon Sobrino challenges the global North to model ministry on the teachings and actions of Jesus. The true service of Jesus involves the complete conversion of the heart – to look squarely at the plight of the poor. This is precisely the ministry of Jesus – to get down on the floor and wash the feet of the poor.[22] 'Such a transformation requires a desacralization and a declericalization of ecclesial ministry'.[23] In other words, the powers-that-be must learn to step down and act with a compassion inspired by Jesus' praxis. As A. E. Orobator holds, '… wherever clericalism provides the norm for leadership there emerges a generalized lack of participation or dialogue involving the lay members of the church'.[24]

Women are being excluded because of their gender instead of being admitted on the merits of their gifts which are vital to the advent of the reign of God. The early Christian community operated in the 'Spirit' and welcomed the gifts of the Spirit active in all members of the community. Women and men exercised their pastoral and spiritual gifts accordingly as teachers, preachers, visionaries, prophets, healers, exorcists, and community leaders. Exercising these gifts had little to do with gender.

Ecclesial ministries today are growing and expanding, albeit still tightly controlled by the hierarchy. The women in the global North have come a long way in being incorporated into ministries; this is in contrast to their sisters in the global South, who are prevented from sharing this same privilege. Ironically, women in the global South know and experience poverty intimately and are closest to the grassroots problems of the poor: African women bear the burden of caring for starving children; African women are raped and abused by warring tribal entities; African women walk hundreds of miles to refugee camps; African women struggle with the ravages of HIV/AIDS.[25] African women, like the Samaritan woman, yearn for 'living waters' from Christ. Should not those who experience the greatest thirst be allowed a sip of life-giving water?

Sadly, women in the global South carry twin burdens in their water jars – oppression and poverty. At the same time, the water in their jars is transformed into the wine of service eked out through pain and suffering.

This wine of service invites the Church to join hands with the Samaritan woman of the South who is asking for living waters to flow to all her sisters and brothers. In this way, ministry of service can become a shared reality and women and men in the Church can come to the table of the Lord as equals – serving and breaking open the bread of compassion.[26]

VII Conclusion: the future is now

Karl Rahner extolled the emergence of a post-Vatican II 'world-Church' liberated from the 'Europeanisms' of a centralized and bureaucratic Church.[27] This new ecclesial reality, at once exciting and terrifying in its demands, owes its origin and existence to the action of the Holy Spirit in the Church and in the world. A less hierarchically structured Church would involve Christians far more deeply in a life of contemplation and protest in the world. Women's yearning for a Church of equality and liberation would be found in communities of equality and discipleship. Here the individual gifts of both women and men will shine unhindered. The role of women will be recognized and appreciated. Authority in the Church will serve the marginalized and downtrodden. Competition for positions of power will give way to service and leadership will pronounce the message of the Gospel. Structures of hierarchy will dissolve into a communion of all the people of God leading gradually to a Church of dialogue and prophetic growth. In this Church, each woman and each man will be a small revelation of the living God manifesting the presence of Jesus Christ.

Notes

1. Elizabeth Moltmann-Wendel and Jürgen Moltmann, *Humanity in God,* Cleveland, OH, 1983, pp. 35–7.
2. Richard McBrien, *The Church: The Evolution of Catholicism*, San Francisco, 2008, pp. 337–43; 345–9.
3. R. McBrien, *The Church*, op. cit., p. 349.
4. Maryknoll, NY, 1986, p. 4.
5. Elizabeth Schüssler Fiorenza, *Wisdom Ways: Introducing Feminist Biblical Interpretation,* "Wo/men's Movements–Wisdom Struggles", Maryknoll, NY, 2006, p. 93.
6. Filomina Chioma Steady, quoted in Rosalyn Terborg-Penn & Andrea Benton Rushing (eds), *Women in Africa and the African Diaspora*, Washington, DC, 1996, p. 4.
7. Teresia M. Hinga, 'Between Colonialism and Inculturation: Feminist Theologies in Africa', in Elisabeth Schüssler Fiorenza (ed.), *The Power of Naming: A Concilium Reader in Feminist Liberation Theology*, Eugene, OR, 2006, p. 42.

8. Jane Fonda, www.youtube.com/topic/Sm6EUR9kSog/miss-representation. Accessed on 26 December 2011.
9. Benedict XVI, *Africae Munus: Post-Synodal Apostolic Exhortation*, 19 November 2011, 41.
10. Elizabeth Johnson, *She Who Is: The Mystery of God in Feminist Theological Discourse*, New York, 1993, p. 38.
11. Elisabeth Schüssler Fiorenza, *Discipleship of Equals: A Critical Feminist Ekklesia-logy of Liberation*, New York, 1993, p. 115.
12. Jon Sobrino, 'The Foundation of All Ministry: Service to the Poor and Victims in a North-South World', in Susan Ross, Maria Clara Bingemer & Paul Murray (eds), *Ministries in the Church*, Concilium 2010/1, p. 17.
13. Bénézet Bujo, *African Theology in its Social Context*, Maryknoll, NY, 1992, pp. 97–8.
14. E. Schüssler Fiorenza, *Discipleship of Equals, op. cit.*, p. 305.
15. Albert Nolan, *Jesus Before Christianity*, Maryknoll, NY, 2004, pp. 148–9.
16. Edward Schllebeeckx, *God is New Each Moment: In Conversation with Huub Oosterhuis and Piet Hoogeveen*, London, 2004, pp. 83–4.
17. Lisa Sowle Cahill, 'The Unity of the Church: Women's Experience', in Giuseppe Reggieri & Miklos Tomka (eds), *The Church in Fragments: Towards What Kind of Unity?*, London & Maryknoll, NY, 1997, 3, p. 95.
18. Diana Hayes, 'Speaking the Future into Life: The Challenge of Black Women in the Church', in Elizabeth Johnson (ed.), *The Church Women Want: Catholic Women in Dialogue*, New York, 2002, p. 84.
19. *Africae Munus* 55.
20. Musimbi R.A Kanyoro, *Introducing Feminist Cultural Hermeneutics: An African Perspective*, New York, 2002, p. 24.
21. Mercy Amba Oduyoye, *Introducing Women's Theology*, Cleveland, OH, 2001, p. 88.
22. J. Sobrino, 'The Foundation of All Ministry', *op. cit.*, pp. 11, 13.
23. E. Schüssler Fiorenza, *Discipleship of Equals, op. cit.*, p. 33.
24. A. E. Orobator, *The Church as Family: African Ecclesiology in its Social Context*, Nairobi, Kenya, 2000, pp. 43–4.
25. Musa Wenkosi Dube, 'John 4:1–42 – The Five Husbands at the Well of Living Waters: The Samaritan Woman and African Women', in Nyambura Njoroge & Musa Dube (eds), *Talitha Cum: Theologies of African Women,* South Africa, 2001, pp. 41–2.
27. Karl Rahner, *Concern for the Church* (Theological Investigations, vol. 20), London, 1981, pp. 77–89.

Part Two: Theological Forum

The Elizabeth A. Johnson Case in the United States

BRADFORD E. HINZE and
CHRISTINE FIRER HINZE

I An ecclesiological perspective

Numerous women theologians have been removed from teaching positions or have been denied approval to teach at Catholic institutions since 1987. Dr Elizabeth Johnson, a member of the Congregation of St Joseph of Brentwood, New York, is the first woman theologian whose work has been publicly criticized by a body of bishops. The details of her case are widely known.[1] The Committee on Doctrine (CoD) of the United States Conference of Catholic Bishops issued a 'Statement on *Quest for the Living God: Mapping Frontiers in the Theology of God*, by Sister Elizabeth A. Johnson' on 24 March 2011. Johnson offered her defence and raised a series of questions to the CoD in a thirty-eight-page set of 'Observations' that was released on 6 June. On 11 October, the CoD responded. Without conceding any point offered in Johnson's defence, and without addressing any of her questions, the bishops reaffirmed their initial assessment of her work and further developed their critique, notably on the question of using female language for God. Dr Johnson offered her final response on 28 October 2011.

The CoD's critique of Johnson's work and the subsequent exchange have sparked wide discussion over many issues, including the nature of revelation, religious language, and the understanding of the Christian doctrine of God, specifically in the areas of Christology and Trinitarian theology.[2] Two further issues have received much attention and merit consideration: the first concerns the nature of theology; the second is ecclesiological.

Johnson's approach to theology represents a leading post-Vatican II effort to embrace an ecclesial Catholicity that is expanding historically and geographically, in order to receive and apply the apostolic faith more effectively, and thereby foster an inclusive ecclesial communion. She has made a highly-responsible attempt to retrieve women's voices, both biblical and historical, as vital resources for the future Catholic understanding of God and the human person; and, by implication, for the pastoral ministry and mission of the Church in the world. Her increasing attentiveness to theological contributions from communities in the southern hemisphere, among immigrant populations in the USA, and especially from women in these local communities, is evidence of a more inclusive geographical catholicity. Johnson's theology is widely recognized as one informed by the living tradition of the Church and the rich symbolic density of the biblical and doctrinal heritage of its faith. She is particularly concerned with Karl Rahner's theology, feminist, liberation, and political theologies, theologies of religious pluralism, and ecological theology. Johnson's method is most clearly apparent in *Quest for the Living God*, and reflects her commitment to honour the witness of faith of the entire people of God. Her theology operates at the frontiers of Catholic theology in ecumenical, interfaith and intercultural contexts.

By contrast, the statements by the CoD in the Johnson case champion a narrower, doctrinaire approach to Catholicity defined in terms of a theology of communion that associates ecclesial unity with a propositional approach to revelation, an a-historical approach to doctrine, and a strict, even legalistic, approach to adherence to the faith as interpreted by the magisterium. The CoD documents epitomize a deductive style reminiscent of the pre-Vatican II theology of neo-scholastic manuals that starts and ends with catechetical and official formulations. The CoD rejects attempts to recover overlooked aspects of the full living tradition of faith in order to inspire a Catholic imagination attuned to the signs of the times, inculturating the Gospel, and promoting social transformation. The CoD's statements are opposed to the use of critical reason in assessing the harmful reception and application of our biblical and doctrinal heritage, and the use of creative imagination and practical reason in developing doctrine.

Widespread protests against the CoD's course of action have concentrated on an ecclesiological issue: the CoD's refusal to engage in any formal dialogue with Dr Johnson about its criticism of her work.[3] Cardinal Donald Wuerl has defended the CoD's action by claiming that it is not bound by the text of the statement approved by the United States

Conference of Catholic Bishops in 1989, *Doctrinal Responsibilities: Approaches to Promoting Cooperation and Resolving Misunderstandings between Bishops and Theologians*, which recommended informal and formal procedures for dialogue between individual bishops and theologians in cases of conflict.[4] The CoD has also been criticized for not complying with *Doctrinal Responsibilities'* assertion of theologians' 'right to a good reputation, and if needed, the defence of that right by appropriate administrative or judicial processes within the Church', and a just procedure consonant with the policy of the Congregation for the Doctrine of the Faith as set forth in the *Regulations for Doctrinal Examination* issued in 1997.[5]

II   A Catholic feminist perspective

'There's something happening here…What it is, ain't exactly clear' is the beginning of a classic US protest song of the late 1960s that seems appropriate to the 2011 exchange between the US Bishops' CoD and Sister Johnson. Their respective positions are clear enough but disturbing aspects of the exchange seem to indicate that there is more to it than is immediately apparent. Full clarity will come only with the passing of time, but a Catholic feminist analysis suggests that the Johnson case is located directly above what might be called the shifting tectonic plates of gender and power relationships within the Catholic community of the present era. It is certainly necessary to address the tension, confusion and eventual failure of these communications between bishops and theologians regarding the 'common faith of the Catholic Church'.

That this author's work has been singled out for episcopal rebuke is both surprising and understandable. After all, Johnson and her work are self-consciously and firmly grounded in the faith of the Catholic Church. She is exceptional among her peers because of her consistent exploration of the frontiers of Christian feminist theology and praxis on the basis of her Roman Catholic faith. Her writing combines intellectual depth and critical rigour with contagious devotion to, and delight in, the living God encountered through the creed, code, and cult of her Catholic tradition. When Johnson's feminist vision and commitments have led her to contest elements of Catholic tradition or practice, she has done so in order to stay close to the heart of that tradition: loving union with the God of Jesus Christ. The result is the characteristically critical and prophetic, yet generous and Catholic style of her theology as fully displayed in *Quest*.

Nevertheless, Johnson's successful inclusion of the perspectives of feminist and liberationist theology in an informed and appreciative account of Catholic tradition, and her ability to communicate with diverse audiences throughout the world, may have provoked the CoD's investigation and public critique. It probably also reacted as it did because the author and subject-matter of *Quest* exemplify shifts and tremors that have unsettled older relationships between bishops and theologians, and between the ordained hierarchy and the laity. The bishops' reply to Johnson's 'Observations' betrays their concern about changes in traditional ways of understanding divine and human identity and power in relation to gender which her investigations foretell. This is clear from the critique of *Quest*'s treatment of God-language, which is also the central theme of Johnson's ground-breaking work of 1993, *She Who Is*.[6]

Destabilizing tensions with regard to authority and power and a male-exclusive hierarchical magisterium help to explain a number of otherwise curious aspects of the bishops' statements. When criticizing Johnson's treatment of analogy as a purely negative stance that occludes the Church's preference for certain God-language, which it insists is divinely-revealed, the CoD twice culls quotations from *Quest* that excise Johnson's articulation of the third stage of analogy as a moment of affirmation and mystical encounter with the Divine.[7] Moreover, Johnson writes that feminists challenge the patriarchal social effects of an exclusive use of male God-language, yet the bishops accuse Johnson of a thoroughgoing (and heterodox) antipathy toward all traditional male imagery for God. When Johnson draws on Scripture, tradition, and the lives of the faithful to elevate and celebrate a wealth of affirmative God-language, both feminine and otherwise, the bishops' negative conclusion, in spite of Johnson's explicit statements, is that *Quest* advocates discarding or replacing traditional male imagery for God. The CoD concludes that, even though Johnson's intention is to write in accordance with the mandate of *Dei verbum* 8, her 2007 book 'in fact fails to fulfil this task, because it does not sufficiently ground itself in the Catholic theological tradition as its starting point'.[8] This apparent episcopal resistance to listening receptively for the voice of the living God at the frontiers limned by *Quest* conceals major differences between the CoD and Johnson concerning just what 'the faith of the Church' and its adequate, authoritative expression comprise and demand.

To interpret the CoD's actions as a straightforward exercise of the hierarchy's responsibility to protect doctrinal orthodoxy, or, conversely, as 'patriarchal boys' disciplining an 'upstart girl' would be to over-simplify the case. Furthermore, it would not be fair to conclude that the bishops' strenuous appeal to divine revelation in order to underscore their claim that 'some' (male) language for God is irreplaceable and enjoys primacy over any other (that is, all non-masculine) language, is a mere attempt to shore up a traditional assumption ('God is more Boy than Girl') that provides crucial ideological support for a male-only priesthood and magisterium. Nevertheless, much more is at issue here than one author's contested ideas about the theology of God. When the bishops reject Johnson's amply-documented claim that, on key contested points, *Quest* articulates 'the same faith of the Church, but in different words',[9] perhaps they do so because they too recognize that language shapes life and practice, and that 'structural change and linguistic change go hand in hand'.[10] In that case, the way in which the bishops have proceeded against Dr Elizabeth Johnson reflects not only major shifts in ecclesial and theological tectonic plates, but all the associated disturbances.

Notes

1. See 'The Elizabeth Johnson Dossier', in R. R. Gaillardetz (ed.), *When the Magisterium Intervenes: The Magisterium and Theologians in Today's Church*, Collegeville, MN, 2012, pp. 177–294.
2. C. L. H. Traina, F. Schüssler Fiorenza, R. Masson & R. R. Gaillardetz, 'Theological Roundtable: The Johnson Case and the Practice of Theology: An Interim Report', *Horizons* 38 (2011), pp. 284–337.
3. For further analysis, see R. R. Gaillardetz, 'Reflections on Key Ecclesiological Issues Raised in the Elizabeth Johnson Case', in *When the Magisterium Intervenes, op. cit.*, pp. 276–94.
4. Cardinal D. Wuerl, 'Bishops as Teachers: A Resource for Bishops', in *When the Magisterium Intervenes, op. cit.*, pp. 201–10, esp. 209.
5. For analysis, see F. A. Sullivan, 'Developments in Teaching Authority since Vatican II', *Theological Studies* 73:3 (2012), forthcoming.
6. E. A. Johnson, *She Who Is: The Mystery of God in Feminist Theological Discourse*, New York, 1993.
7. Committee on Doctrine, 'Response to Observations', in *When The Magisterium Intervenes, op. cit.*, pp. 262–3, quoting E. A. Johnson, *Quest for the Living God*, New York, 2007, pp. 18–9.
8. 'Response to Observations', in *When the Magisterium Intervenes, op. cit.,* pp. 259–60, esp. 260.
9. E. A. Johnson, 'Observations,' in *When the Magisterium Intervenes, op. cit.*, p. 230; Committee on Doctrine, 'Response to Observations', *ibid.*, p. 260.
10. *She Who Is, op. cit.*, p. 40.

What is Reality? Situating an Ontological Question

PAULO SUESS

On 13 May 2007, in his opening address to the fifth General Conference of Latin American and Caribbean Bishops at Aparecida, Pope Benedict XVI asked if giving priority to faith in Christ could be an escape from reality and the real world into a spiritual world. 'What is this "reality"? What is real?' asked the Pope and gave his answer: 'Those who exclude God from their horizon falsify the concept of "reality"…Only the person who recognizes God knows reality and can respond to it in an adequate and really human way.' In other words, atheists and agnostics cannot be true humanists or respond adequately to reality. But this seems open to question, since Vatican II took a positive view of the autonomy of earthly reality, for, it said, 'by the very nature of creation material being is endowed with its own stability, truth and excellence, its own order and laws' (*Gaudium et spes* 36). And *Gaudium et spes* continues: 'Consequently methodical research in all branches of knowledge, provided it is carried out in a truly scientific manner and does not override moral laws, can never conflict with the faith, because the things of the world and the things of faith derive from the same God' (*Gaudium et spes* 36; cf. 75).

Moreover, according to the Christian view, scientists with no link to any religious denomination work with the 'prejudice' of the existence of Him of Whom every person can state with Augustine: 'He is closer to me than my innermost self' (cf. *Confessions* III,6,11). God constitutes the true interiority and identity of the human being and the world. Consequently, 'openness to the world', to reality and to human beings is, implicitly, always openness to God, which may be made explicit or not. The Church itself is part of this world, this reality and this humanity.

The autonomy of earthly realities allows us to distinguish two levels, natural and supernatural, without separation or confusion (Chalcedon: *indivise, inconfuse*). In a first attempt to analyse reality, we have to examine its scientific criteria. There is no reason in any such analysis to bring in interpretations based on selective faith criteria that vary from one religious denomination to another. The temporal order is autonomous in relation to the order of the spiritual and of salvation. This is a premiss of the secular state, which does not depend on the different factions of believers it administers, although they may collaborate at different levels to ensure the smooth running of the *res publica*.

In asserting the priority of a theological vision for any situation analysis, the Pope was replying indirectly to a manoeuvre undertaken during the fourth General Conference of Latin American and Caribbean Bishops in Santo Domingo in 1992. In the final stage of drafting of the conference's 'Final Text', an 'invisible hand' rearranged the text overnight, replacing the 'see' section, the situation analysis, by a theological reflection on 'Jesus Christ, Gospel of the Father'. The socio-economic situation analysis did not disappear completely. It was shortened, inserted as small segments throughout the text, and subordinated to faith criteria without any analytical justification.

This intervention resulted in a new version of the text and disturbed the majority of delegates. That same morning, the conference in plenary assembly was informed that the standing orders did not allow any further changes to the text altered during the night. In Aparecida, the Pope implicitly approved the overnight procedure. Situation analysis would have to give priority to data from faith, though without subsequently excluding empirical data from the social sciences. Ever since Santo Domingo, the majority of Latin American church documents have begun with a theological reflection, followed by empirical data about the context. The 'new vision' gives faith statements an almost scientific status; it abandons the original 'see, judge, act' methodology that, since Medellín, had been the trademark of church documents in Latin America and the Caribbean, and confuses different levels of analysis.

The 'see, judge, act' methodology originated in the Young Christian Workers (YCW), founded by Father Pierre Cardijn in Belgium in 1925, and in the world of the French worker priests. The worker-priest experiment, supported by bishops (Liénart, Suhard) and theologians (Chenu, Congar), was banned by Pius XII in 1954. Pius' successor, John XXIII (1958–63), in his ground-breaking encyclical *Mater et magistra*

(1961), recognized the 'see, judge, act' methodology as a valid instrument of social analysis: 'Doctrinal principles on social matters are frequently put into effect in three stages: first there is a survey to discover the real state of affairs, then this state of affairs is carefully compared with the principles, and finally there is a decision on what action can or should be undertaken to adapt traditional norms to a particular time and place. These three stages are often described by the following verbs: 'see, judge, act' (*Mater et magistra* 236).

As a whole, John XXIII's pontificate endorsed a new commitment of the Church to the world and its realities. Slogans such *aggiornamento* and 'signs of the times' (cf. *Pacem in terris* 39ff) found a clear echo at the Second Vatican Council (cf. *Gaudium et spes* 11). Paul VI, in his encyclical *Ecclesiam suam* (1964), recalled John XXIII's use of the word *aggiornamento* and described it as the 'guiding principle' of the Council (*Ecclesiam suam* 50).

The Latin American bishops' conferences of Medellín (1968) and Puebla (1979) remained faithful to the principles of *aggiornamento* and the 'autonomy of earthly realities', preferring to put the 'judging' of the temporal order by faith criteria in second place and to give 'theological illumination' not priority but a central role.

The intervention in the 'Final Text' of Santo Domingo featured the reappearance of an historic dispute between two schools of theology, St Augustine's Platonism and St Thomas Aquinas' Aristotelianism. In the conquest of the Americas, these two positions represented theological references that had a direct influence on the treatment of the indigenous peoples. The first group took their stand on the twelfth-century 'theology of sentences', with its theocratic vision of papal power and pessimistic view of human nature; the second relied on the natural-law position developed by Aquinas in the thirteenth century. In referring to the laws of the Junta of Burgos, which in 1512 produced legislation on the status of the indigenous that was detrimental to the position of those peoples, Bartolomé de Las Casas mentioned that it contained 'Hostiensis' error'. Las Casas' Hostiensis was Henrico da Susa (d. 1270), an Italian decretalist, who defended the thesis that 'by the very coming of Christ into the world, *ipso jure* or *ipso facto*, all infidels were deprived of their lordships, jurisdictions, dignities, honours, kingdoms and States'. To refute Hostiensis' thesis, Las Casas wrote his treatise *On the only way of calling all pagans to the true religion*.[1]

Peter Lombard's 'theology of sentences', for example, exhibited a certain confusion between the natural and supernatural orders. Following the tradition of St Augustine (354–430), when combating Pelagianism, which denied original sin and the need for infant baptism, the 'sentencialists' attributed to original sin an influence that almost destroys human nature. Consequently, there is a need for a counterweight in the form of grace and the supernatural. The minimization of the natural inspired theocratic interpretations of papal power as early as the time of Gregory VII (1073–85).

By the thirteenth century, something new had emerged in the universities of Paris, Bologna, Oxford and Salamanca. Aristotle (still banned by the Church at the beginning of the century) was translated through the influence of the Arabs, and reading him helped theology to recognize the limits of its competence. Thomas Aquinas (1225–74), freely inspired by Aristotle, advanced theological thinking when he began to distinguish between the natural and the supernatural, between reason and faith. Just as the natural does not dispense with grace (the supernatural), so grace does not destroy nature but perfects it. Divine law, which has its origin in grace, does not suspend human law, which belongs to the order of nature.[2]

Vatican II's theology of earthly realities represented a victory for Thomas Aquinas and his natural-law school. The Council accepted religious liberty and pluralism as human rights; before Vatican II they were considered acceptable only *de facto*, not *de jure*, because 'error' could be allowed no rights. Nevertheless the post-conciliar period has been increasingly marked by the Pentecostal euphoria of small groups and by the authoritarian pessimism of a variety of neo-Augustinianism. Once again, religious liberty in its form of religious pluralism is being questioned as a 'relativist' theory that seeks to justify itself 'not only *de facto* but also *de jure*, (or *in principle*)'.[3] In a world of great changes, a significant sector of the Catholic Church is running the risk of reducing John XXIII's *aggiornamento* to a conservative modernization inspired by the question: 'How can we adapt to the world without changing substantially?' If it puts off the 'pastoral conversion' advocated by Aparecida (365ff), the so-called New Evangelization also runs this risk.

These 'fragments' show us the interweaving of 'reality', 'world' and 'human being', and humans not in the abstract but in their specificity as poor and other. In their homes and their territories, which are in the front line of conflicts central to the world, we come to see the appeals of reality and the commitments to it which we are required to make (cf. Aparecida 491) if our faith is to be incarnate.

If the Pope in Germany, at his 'Meeting with Catholics engaged in the Church and society', proposed that the Church should 'become unworldly', he was thus not proposing a withdrawal from the realities of the world, but 'a profound liberation of the Church from forms of worldliness': in other words, from superficialities, that is, from 'material and political burdens and privileges' that are opposed to the Gospel. The Church as it were, sets aside its 'worldly wealth and once again completely embraces its worldly poverty'. 'Worldly poverty', as a mere ascetic exercise, could become 'an escape from reality into a spiritual world', if this poverty did not have specific faces and a clear task: to make the poor Church 'the house of the poor' (Aparecida 8; cf. 524). The Church's option for 'worldly poverty' is the premiss of the option for the poor. Evangelization that starts from the option for the poor, who represent Jesus crucified in history, can be the Ariadne's thread leading us through the labyrinth of reality and the world, and at the same time the lodestar of the 'new evangelization'.

Translated by Francis McDonagh

Notes

1. Bartolomé de Las Casas, *De unico vocationis modo omnium gentium ad veram religionem*, México, 1942–75. Cf. Las Casas, *Historia de las Indias*, vol. 2, México, 1981, III, ch. 57 e 7.
2. Cf. Thomas Aquinas, *Summa Theologica* II.2, q. 104, art. 6; II.2. q; 10, art. 10. Cf Paulo Suess, 'Liberdade e servidão. Missionários, juristas e teólogos espanhóis do século XVI frente à causa indígena', in Suess (ed.), *Queimada e semeadura*, Petrópolis, 1988, pp. 21–44, specifically 32ff for the principle referred to: 'Jus divinum, quod est ex gratia, non tollit jus humanum quod est ex naturali ratione'.
3. Congregation for the Doctrine of the Faith, Declaration *Dominus Iesus* (2000) 4.
4. Benedict XVI, Address during his Apostolic Visit to Germany. Meeting with Catholics engaged in the Life of the Church and Society, Freiburg im Breisgau, 25 September 2011: http://www.vatican.va/holy_father/benedict_xvi/speeches/2011/september/documents/hf_ben-xvi_spe_20110925_catholics-freiburg_en.html.

The Arab Spring Muslim Non-violence as a Sign of the Times

DREW CHRISTIANSEN SJ

Among the signs of hope we should also count the spread . . . of a new sensitivity ever more opposed to war as an instrument of resolution of conflicts between peoples, and increasingly oriented to find effective but 'non-violent' means to counter the armed aggressor.[1]

I Secular surprise

In December 2010 a street vendor named Mohamed Bouazizi set himself ablaze in the Tunisian town of Sisi Bouzid and ushered in the Arab Spring, a series of popular uprisings against autocratic governments across the Arab lands. Bouazizi had been driven to desperation by police harassment and extortion that made it impossible for him to ply his trade. But his death coincided with the conclusion of two years of planning by activists in Tunisia and Egypt for concerted non-violent protests for democracy against their countries' autocratic regimes.[2] In 28 days, Zine El Abidine Ben Ali, the Tunisian President, fled to exile in Saudi Arabia, and within seventeen days of protests breaking out in Cairo, Hosni Mubarak, President of Egypt, retired to his villa at Sharm el Sheikh, where he was soon put under house arrest.

Neither governments nor scholars anticipated such dramatic change, nor non-violent change led by secular and progressive Muslim activists. Demonstrations swept across the region: Libya, Yemen, Bahrain, Jordan, Syria and Morocco.[3] (For first-hand accounts of Egypt's revolution, see A. Khalil, *Liberation Square: Inside the Egyptian Revolution and the Rebirth of a Nation,* New York, 2012, and W. Ghonim, *Revolution 2.0: The Power of the People is Greater Than the People in Power,* Boston, 2012). The protestors frequently struggled to sustain non-violent campaigns in the face of repression. At the time of writing this article, elections have taken place in Tunisia, Egypt and Morocco.

II Non-violent campaigns

The cadres of activists who launched the Jasmin Revolution in Tunisia and Egypt were aided by Qatar's Academy of Change, a think tank that popularized the ideas of the American non-violent theorist Gene Sharp. The cadres' blue-print was Sharp's monograph *From Dictatorship to Democracy*.[4] In Libya, Bahrain and Syria, with no trained cadres among the population prepared for peaceful resistance, the people nevertheless sustained their non-violent protests week after week in the face of the armed force used against them.

It was months before the protestors called for outside intervention, and longer before international bodies intervened: the UN and NATO in Libya, and the Arab League in Syria. It was months longer before the protest movements began to resort to armed resistance in Libya or to incorporate military defectors in the Syrian resistance. When the Syrian National Council, the leading exile group, united with the Free Syrian Army, a grouping of Syrian military defectors, the FSA accepted the primacy of the Council and its non-violent agenda.[5]

III Muslim non-violence

Muslim societies have sustained non-violent movements before.[6] In the late nineteenth and early twentieth centuries, Arab Muslim populations of the Ottoman Empire conducted non-violent resistance against the secularizing policies of the Young Turks. In the mid-twentieth century, Abdul Ghaffar Khan, 'the Frontier Gandhi', worked for Indian independence. For five years in the 1930s, urban elites in Palestine led the Great Arab Revolt against the British Mandate as a non-violent campaign, culminating in the General Strike of 1936.[7] More recently, Muslim thinkers have begun to make a case for non-violence. Arsalan Iftikhar premisses the Muslim argument for non-violence on the oneness of *Allah*, the unity of 'the sons of Adam' and the primacy of forgiveness, compassion and mercy in Islamic ethics.[8]

For social science, non-violent direct action is a broad secular trend in which religion and religiously-based social movements play a role.[9] For its part, contemporary Catholic social teaching regards non-violence as one of the 'signs of the times'.[10] Often practised by religious leaders such as Dorothy Day and Martin Luther King, churches like the Mennonites, and religiously-inspired movements such as the Catholic Peace Fellowship, in recent decades non-violence has experienced explosive growth among non-governmental organizations, such as the Academy of Change, and in new social movements, such as the Egyptian April 6 Movement.[11]

IV A Catholic perspective on Muslim non-violence

In modern Catholic social teaching, the warrant for non-violence as a public ethical stance is a relatively recent phenomenon.[12] The Second Vatican Council offered grudging praise for 'those who renounce the use of violence...and resort to methods of defence that are otherwise available to weaker parties...'.[13] The phrasing implied that non-violent resistance is an exceptional activity. Change came only after the fall of Communism to non-violent revolutions in Eastern Europe in 1989. Reflecting on those events in his 1991 encyclical *Centesimus annus*, the late Pope John Paul II attributed the transformation of European politics to persistent non-violent activity, and recommended non-violent strategies in domestic and in international conflicts.[14]

Pope John Paul II, of course, had served as a guide to the Polish resistance movement Solidarity, and in 1989, had negotiated with Mikhail Gorbachev, the President of the Soviet Union, to forestall a Soviet invasion of Eastern Europe. Subsequently, Pope Benedict XVI has also endorsed non-violence.[15] Although non-violence has not been a topic in formal Muslim-Catholic dialogue, the renunciation of violence by the world's religions has been a constant theme at convocations of religious leaders, including Muslims, called in Assisi by Pope John Paul II and Pope Benedict XVI, particularly in 1993 during the war in Bosnia, and in 2002 after the invasion of Afghanistan.

Nevertheless, the official Catholic response to the Arab Spring has been cautious because of well-founded anxiety about the persecution of native Arab Christians in the wake of the Muslim advances in open elections. But it is undeniable that the goals that inspire the movements (human dignity, self-government, the rule of law, non-violent political change, and sometimes religious pluralism) are also the aspirations which recent Catholic social teaching has identified as signs of the times. Therefore, although political prudence may be necessary to safeguard the future of the Church in the Middle East, it would be a mistake to conflate the Arab Spring with extremist activities that exploit the political space opened up by the uprisings for sectarian ends. The persistent non-violence of the Arab masses over many months must be acknowledged, like the 1989 Eastern European revolutions, as evidence, in John Paul II's words, of 'the non-violent commitment of people, who, while always refusing to yield to the force of power, succeeded time after time in effective ways of bearing witness to truth'.[16] Furthermore, the non-violence of the Arab Spring may offer an opportunity for discussions with Muslims about common values consistent with Pope Benedict's pleas to place human rights and shared values on the agenda of interreligious dialogues.

Notes

1. John Paul II, *Evangelium vitae* (The Gospel of Life), Vatican City, 1995, 27.
2. 'Egyptians and Tunisians Collaborated to Shake Arab History', *New York Times*, 14 February 2011.
3. For a survey of the nations affected by the Arab Spring and the variations of Islam in each, see E. Mallon, 'Will Democracy Bloom?', *America*, 10 October 2011. For an interim report on Bahrain, Egypt and Libya, see M. Fisher, 'New Realities after a Revolution', *Washington Post*, 21 December 2011.
4. 'Shy US Intellectual Created a Playbook Used in a Revolution', *New York Times*, 16 February 2011; 'Gene Sharp Navigator', *New York Times*, 17 December 2011.
5. 'Syrian opposition groups agree to coordinate efforts', *Los Angeles Times*, 21 December 2011.
6. For counter-Jihadist cultural trends in the Muslim worlds, see R. Wright, *Rock the Casbah: Rage and Rebellion across the Islamic World* (New York, 2011); 'In Protests, Syrians Find the Spark of Creativity', *New York Times*, 20 December 2011.
7. Chapter 4 of A. Iftikhar, *Islamic Pacifism: Global Muslims in the Post-Osama Era*, Amazon/CreateSpace, 2011, summarizes the history of these non-violent Muslim movements.
8. Iftikhar's argument, though not yet widely accepted, offers an Islamic rationale for the non-violence practised in the Arab Spring.
9. For social-science views on the decline of violence, see J. S. Goldstein, *Winning the War on War: The Decline of Armed Conflict Worldwide,* New York, 2011; S. Pinker, *The Better Angels of Our Nature: Why Violence Has Declined*, New York, 2011.
10. See especially John XXIII, *Pacem in terris* (Peace on Earth), 126–9, and Vatican II, *Gaudium et spes* (The Pastoral Constitution on the Church in the Modern World) 82, in D. J. O'Brien & T. A. Shannon (eds), *Catholic Social Thought: The Documentary Heritage*, Maryknoll, NY, 1992.
11. On contemporary Catholic peace programmes, see R. J. Schreiter, R. S. Appleby & G.

F. Powers (eds), *Peacebuilding: Catholic Theology, Ethics and Praxis,* Maryknoll, NY, 2010.
12. On the history and forms of Catholic pacifism and non-violence, see R. Musto, *The Catholic Peace Tradition*, Maryknoll, NY, 1986.
13. *Gaudium et spes* 78.
14. Pope John Paul II, *Centesimus annus* (On the Hundredth Anniversary of *Rerum novarum)*, 23, 25 & 52, in *Catholic Social Thought, op. cit.*
15. Angelus talks, 18 February 2007 and 3 July 2011.
16. *Centesimus annus, op. cit.*, 23.

Contributors

REGINA AMMICHT QUINN studied Catholic Theology and German Literature. She is a Professor at the International Centre for Ethics in Science (IZEW), University of Tübingen. Her publications include: *Von Lissabon bis Auschwitz: Zum Paradigmawechsel in der Theodizeefrage*, Freiburg im Bresigau, 1992; *Körper, Religion und Sexualität: Theologische Reflexion zur Ethik der Geschlechter*, Mainz ³2004; *Glück – der Ernst des Lebens*, Freiburg i. Br., 2006; 'Living with Losses: The Crisis in the "Christian West"', in James F. Keenan (ed.): *Catholic Theological Ethics: Past, Present, and Future*, New York, 2011.

Email: regina.ammicht-quinn@t-online.de

JADRANKA REBEKA ANIĆ is a research associate at the Ivo Pilar Institute of Social Science in Split (Croatia). She is the Chair of the Croat section of the European Association of Women for Theological Research. Her publications include a book on understanding gender, a history of a debate and varying interpretations of the concept in the Church.

Email: rebeka.anic@pilar.hr

ANNE ARABOME SSS is a visiting scholar at the Program of African Studies at Northwestern University in Evanston. She is a member of the Sisters of Social Service of Los Angeles, CA. She holds a Doctor of Ministry degree in Spirituality from the Catholic Theological Union in Chicago. Her research interest includes ethical and theological issues that shape the spiritual lives of African women.

Email: omoye208@yahoo.co.uk

Contributors

LISA SOWLE CAHILL is Professor of Theology, Boston College, USA. Her books include *Theological Bioethics: Participation, Justice and Change* (Georgetown), *Sex, Gender and Christian Ethics* (Cambridge) and *Global Justice, Christology and Christian Ethics* (Cambridge, forthcoming).

Email: cahilll@bc.edu

DREW CHRISTIANSEN SJ is Editor-in-chief of the US Jesuit weekly *America*. For 14 years, he advised the US Catholic bishops on Middle East policy.

Email: DrewC33299@aol.com

HEATHER EATON is a full Professor at Saint Paul University, Ottawa. She is engaged in religious responses to the ecological crisis, ecological, feminist and liberation theologies, and connections between religion and science. Recent work concerns the intersection of religion, evolution and ecology, peace and conflict studies on gender, ecology and religion, and animal rights.

Email: theology@ustpaul.ca

BENEDITO FERRARO **is** Professor of Theology at the Pontifical Catholic University of Campinas, São Paulo, Brazil, specializing in Christology and the Trinity. He is a National Inspector of base communities in Brazil, a member of the continental base community organization, and President of the CESEP (Ecumenical Centre for Evangelization and Popular Education.

Email: bferraro@terra.com.br

PATRICIA FOX teaches in the theology department at Flinders University of South Australia. She also developed and implemented a Ministry Formation Programme for Lay Ecclesial Ministers and Permanent Deacons

Contributors

based at Catholic Theological College, Adelaide Theological Centre, Brooklyn Park, SA.

Email: pt.fox@flinders.edu.au

BRADFORD E. HINZE is Associate Chair for Graduate Studies at Fordham University in New York.

Email: bhinze@fordham.edu

CHRISTINE FIRER HINZE is Co-Director of The Francis and Ann Curran Center for American Catholic Studies at Fordham University in New York.

Email: hinze@fordham.edu

DIEGO IRARRAZAVAL is a member of the Board of Directors and the Board of Editors of *Concilium*. He teaches and exercises his ministry in Santiago, Chile. He is the author of *Teologia en la fe del pueblo*, *Inculturacion, Un Jesus Jovial,* and other writings.

Email: diegoira@hotmail.com

LUIS CORREA LIMA SJ is a Jesuit priest, holds a doctorate in history and is Professor at the Catholic Pontifical University of Rio de Janeiro. He specializes in the history of the Church and the modern world. His publications are in the fields of moral theology and economics of the sixteenth century, and long-duration history and structures.

Email: lclima@puc-rio.br

MURIEL OREVILLO-MONTENEGRO is a Professor of theology at Silliman University (Dumagete City, Philippines), where she served as the first woman Dean of the Divinity School. She received her STM and PhD.

from Union Theological Seminary in New York City, and is the author of *The Jesus of Asian Women*.

Email: muriel.orevillomontenegro@gmail.com

PAULO SUESS is a diocesan priest and doctor in fundamental theology. He has worked in the Amazon region since 1966, and from 1979 to 1983, he was Secretary General of the Indigenist Missionary Council (CIMI). He is a former President of the International Association for Mission Studies (IAMS). He is currently theological adviser to CIMI and Comina (National Missionary Council). Paulo Suess is also Professor in the post-graduate department of the São Paulo Institute of Higher Studies (ITESP), and the author of various books.

Email: suess@uol.com.br

ELSA TAMEZ is Professor Emerita of the Latin American Biblical University and is currently adviser on translations to the Sociedades Bíblicas Unidas. Her publications include *La Biblia de los oprimidos, Contra toda –condena. La justificación por la fédes de los excluidos, El movimiento de Jesús y las mujeres, Luchas de poder en los orígenes del cristianismo,* and a study of the First Letter to Timothy.

Email: elsa.tamez@gmail.com

SUSAN ST VILLE is Director of the Master's Program at the Kroc Institute for International Peace Studies, University of Notre Dame, and a clinician whose private practice focuses on trauma-related disorders. She is the co-editor (with Ellen Armour) of *Bodily Citations: Religionists Engage Judith Butler.*

Email: Susan.M.StVille.2@nd.edu

Concilium Subscription Information

February   2013/1: *Reconciliation: Empowering Grace*

April   2013/2: *Postcolonial Theology*

August   2013/3: *Saints and Sanctity Today*

October   2013/4: *The Ambivalence of Sacrifice*

December   2013/5: *Orthodoxy*

New subscribers: to receive *Concilium 2013* (five issues) anywhere in the world, please copy this form, complete it in block capitals and send it with your payment to the dress below.

Please enter my subscription for *Concilium 2013*

Individuals
____ £50 UK
____ £72 overseas and Eire
____ $95 North America/Rest of World
____ €85 Europe

Institutions
____ £72 UK
____ £92 overseas and Eire
____ $110 North America/Rest of World
____ €135 Europe

Postage included – airmail for overseas subscribers

Payment Details:
Payment must accompany all orders and can be made by cheque or credit card
I enclose a cheque for £/$/€ ____ Payable to Hymns Ancient and Modern Ltd
Please charge my Visa/MasterCard (Delete as appropriate) for £/$/€ ____

Credit card number _____

Expiry date _____

Signature of cardholder _____

Name on card _____

Telephone _____ E-mail _____

Send your order to *Concilium,* **Hymns Ancient and Modern Ltd**
13a Hellesdon Park Road, Norwich NR6 5DR, UK
E-mail: concilium@hymnsam.co.uk
or order online at www.conciliumjournal.co.uk

Customer service information
All orders must be prepaid. Subscriptions are entered on an annual basis (i.e. January to December). No refunds on subscriptions will be made after the first issue of the Journal has been despatched. If you have any queries or require Information about other payment methods, please contact our Customer Services department.

CONCILIUM
International Journal of Theology

FOUNDERS
Anton van den Boogaard; Paul Brand; Yves Congar, OP; Hans Küng;
Johann Baptist Metz; Karl Rahner, SJ; Edward Schillebeeckx

BOARD OF DIRECTORS
President: Felix Wilfred
Vice Presidents: Erik Borgman; Diego Irarrázaval; Susan Ross

BOARD OF EDITORS
Regina Ammicht Quinn (Frankfurt, Germany)
Mike Babić
Maria Clara Bingemer (Rio de Janeiro, Brazil)
Erik Borgman (Nijmegen, The Netherlands)
Lisa Sowle Cahill (Boston, USA)
Frère Thierry Marie Courau (France)
Hille Haker (Frankfurt, Germany)
Diego Irarrázaval (Santiago, Chile)
Solange Lefebvre (Montreal, Canada)
Eloi Messi Metogo (Yaounde, Cameroon)
Sarojini Nadar (Durban, South Africa)
Daniel Franklin Pilario (Quezon City, Philippines)
Susan Ross (Chicago, USA)
Silvia Scatena (Reggio Emilia, Italy)
Jon Sobrino SJ (San Salvador, El Salvador)
Luiz Carlos Susin (Porto Alegre, Brazil)
Andres Torres Queiruga (Santiago de Compostela, Spain)
João J. Viba-Chã (Portugal)
Marie-Theres Wacker (Münster, Germany)
Felix Wilfred (Madras, India)

PUBLISHERS
SCM Press (London, UK)
Matthias-Grünewald Verlag (Ostfildern, Germany)
Editrice Queriniana (Brescia, Italy)
Editorial Verbo Divino (Estella, Spain)
EditoraVozes (Petropolis, Brazil)
Ex Libris and Synopsis (Rijeka, Croatia)

Concilium Secretariat:
Asian Centre for Cross-Cultural Studies,
40/6A, Panayur Kuppam Road, Sholinganallur Post, Panayur, Madras 600119, India.
Phone: +91- 44 24530682 Fax: +91- 44 24530443
E-mail: Concilium.madras@gmail.com
Managing Secretary: Arokia Mary Anthonidas

New Titles from SCM Press

Diagonal Advance
Perfection in Christian Theology
ANTHONY D. BAKER

Diagonal Advance argues for a radical revision of Christian thinking about the purpose of human life. Perfection is neither a vertical drop from the divine, nor a horizontal progression through social and personal development. Rather, it is a diagonal advance into the divine perfections through the perfecting of material culture.

Through a critical engagement with contemporary texts, concluding with a dramatic revision of the Prometheus mythology, the author argues for a renewed diagonalizing of Christian perfection.

978 0334 04180 1   Paperback   £50.00

Ethics of Hope
JURGEN MOLTMANN

Jurgen Moltmann is Professor emeritus of Systematic Theology at the University of Tubingen, Germany. He is one of the most important post-war, post-Holocaust theologians whose work has influenced the last two generations of theological thought in Germany and worldwide.

Building on the conviction, asserted in his *Theology of Hope*, that Christian existence and social matters are inextricably tied together in the political sphere, Moltmann unfolds his ethics of hope in light of eschatology, clearly distinguishing it from prior and competing visions of Christian ethics. In the process, he applies this framework to concrete issues of medical ethics, ecological ethics, and just-war ethics.

978 0334 04403 1   Paperback   £40.00

Available in all good bookshops
Alternatively order direct from the publisher on
+44(0)1603 785 925 or online at www.scmpress.co.uk

www.ingramcontent.com/pod-product-compliance
Lightning Source LLC
Chambersburg PA
CBHW051403290426
44108CB00015B/2137